A STUDENTS GUIDE TO THE RULE AGAINST PERPETUITIES

Frederic S. Schwartz

Associate Professor
Oklahoma City University
School of Law

STUDENT GUIDE SERIES

Matthew Bender

MATTHEW BENDER & CO.
EDITORIAL OFFICES
TWO PARK AVENUE, NEW YORK, NY 10016 (212) 448-2000
201 MISSION STREET, SAN FRANCISCO, CA 94105 (415) 908-3200

3 4 5 6 7 8 9 0 P 0 9 8 7 6 5

(Pub.645)

To my family

Preface
How to use this book

Even if you are just now beginning your study of the Rule against Perpetuities, you might think you already know one thing about it: that it is difficult to learn. There are at least two good reasons for discarding this "knowledge." First, you may conclude that the Rule is not so difficult after all. Second, *thinking* that something is difficult to learn will help make it so. Relax! You might discover, not only that the Rule is less difficult than you expected, but also that it is rather fascinating.

As for the book itself: you may, of course, choose to read it from cover to cover. On the other hand, you may want to skip those parts of the book which are devoted to a review of the law of estates and future interests, if you are confident that you already know that material well. Wherever an understanding of the law of estates and future interests is especially important for an understanding of the Rule against Perpetuities, you will find a cross-reference to the review material.

Each of the principles discussed in this book is illustrated by one or more examples in the text. In addition, there are problems, with answers, at the end of some of the chapters. Use these problems in the way that suits you best. If you are unsure whether you fully understand the discussion in the text, then you may want to use some of the problems, and their answers, as additional examples to read and study. Once you feel more confident about your understanding of the text discussion--or if the discussion seemed clear from the start--you can test yourself by attempting to solve the problems yourself before looking at the answers.

TABLE OF CONTENTS

Chapter 1
Introduction

The Rule against Perpetuities, which is part of the common law of most United States jurisdictions, is the creation of the English courts and an American law professor. The Rule had its beginnings in 17th-century decisions in the English courts, but it continued to evolve in England until the 19th century. In 1886, John Chipman Gray, a teacher of property law at the Harvard Law School, published the first edition of his book, The Rule Against Perpetuities. Gray did not simply restate the law as it had developed in England and the United States; he attempted to clear up various points of confusion and to refine the Rule. So great was Gray's influence that the final development of the Rule must be credited to him. In fact, Gray's one-sentence statement of the Rule is accepted as "the" Rule:

> No interest is good unless it must vest, if at all, not later than twenty-one years after some life in being at the creation of the interest.[1]

So concise is Gray's statement that it gives little clue to what the Rule actually does. Still, you may be able to glean at least one thing from his famous sentence: the Rule invalidates interests which might remain contingent for too long. Attempting to discover the purpose of the Rule is an exercise in frustration. It is usually said that contingent interests fetter the free alienability of property and allow grantors or testators to exert undue control over property after they are dead. However, it is hard to see why many interests which are valid under the Rule are any less a cause of these evils than are many interests which the Rule strikes down.[2]

It is not very important, in most cases, to know the policies (if any) which support the Rule against Perpetuities in order to apply it. What *is* important is to have a good understanding of the law of estates and future interests. Chapter 2 reviews that topic. Even if you are confident that you know that material well, you may want to give the chapter at least a glance. Our review of estates and future interests emphasizes those aspects of the law that are most important for understanding and applying the Rule against Perpetuities.

---

[1]J. Gray, The Rule Against Perpetuities § 201, at 191 (4th ed. 1942).

[2]E. Clark, L. Lusky, and A. Murphy, Cases and Materials on Gratuitous Transfers 744-749 (3d ed. 1985).

1

Chapter 2
Review of estates and future interests

Our discussion of the Rule itself is preceded by a brief review of the general law relating to estates and future interests. Keep in mind that what follows is only a sketch of the broad outlines of the law; many details and qualifications have been omitted.

§ 2.01 Estates in land

The right to possess a particular parcel of land can be sliced up in terms of time. It might be, for example, that a person has the right to possess the land now for a specified period of time, while one or more others have the right to possess the same land in the future. We use the word "estate" to describe the right to possess a parcel of land, now or in the future. In fact, even the *possibility* of having the right to possess the land in the future is an estate. (In the past some such "possibilities" were not considered estates, but nowadays it would not be inappropriate to call them that.)

Someone who has the right to possess the land now is said to have a present estate. If someone has the right to possess in the future (or the possibility of having the right to possess in the future), he has a future estate or, more commonly, a "future interest."

Unfortunately, the single most important characteristic of every "future interest" is misdescribed by the term itself. The various kinds of future interests, like the present estates, are all *presently existing interests*. They can be created, owned, and (for the most part) transferred *now*. The owner of a future interest will be protected in his future right of possession (e.g., by preventing the present possessor from injuring the land) just as the owner of a present estate will be protected in his present right of possession. In short, it is not the *existence* of a future interest that is "future"; it is the *right of possession* which it confers.

In the two sections that follow we review the terms used to describe the various kinds of present estates and future interests.

§ 2.02 Present estates

[A] Fee simple absolute

The "largest" estate is the fee simple absolute; it describes a right of possession which lasts forever. Of course, the mortal owner of a fee simple absolute will not be able, himself, to possess the land forever. But he can make an inter-vivos transfer of it or devise it (transfer it by will), and if he does neither his heirs will inherit it. In this way the right of possession given by the fee simple absolute can, and does, last beyond the owner's lifetime. (If the owner of a fee simple absolute dies without heirs and without devising it, the estate will escheat to the state.)

It used to be necessary, in an inter-vivos conveyance, to use the words "and his heirs" (or "and her heirs") to create a fee simple absolute (or any other kind of fee simple) in the grantee.

Example 2-1
O conveys "to *A* and his heirs."

A has a fee simple absolute. Today, however, the words "and his heirs" are no longer necessary to create a fee simple, and we will not use them in this book.

Example 2-2
O conveys "to *A*."

A has a fee simple absolute.

[B] Fee simple determinable

A transferor may desire that the transferee be entitled to possession only for so long as a specified state of affairs continues or only until some specified event occurs. The transferor's intent to limit the transferee's right of possession in that way might be expressed with language such as "until [a specified event occurs]," "for so long as [a specified state of affairs continues]," or "while [a specified state of affairs continues]." Each one of these phrases, or a similar one, constitutes a "special limitation." The interest itself is called a fee simple on special limitation or, more commonly, a fee simple determinable.

Example 2-3
O conveys "to *A* for so long as the land is used for residential purposes."

A has a fee simple determinable. If and when the land is no longer used for residential purposes, the right of possession returns immediately and automatically to *O*.

[C] Fee simple subject to a condition subsequent

There is another way in which the transferor can express his desire that the transferee be entitled to possession only for so long as a specified state of affairs continues or only until some specified event occurs. A condition expressed with the words "but if," "on the condition that," "provided that," or the like is called a condition subsequent. If the transferor attaches such a condition to a fee simple, he has created a fee simple subject to a condition subsequent.

Example 2-4
O conveys "to *A*, but if the land is not used for residential purposes, *O* may re-enter and re-take his former estate."

A has a fee simple subject to a condition subsequent.

Admittedly, the difference between the kind of language which states a special limitation (which resulted in the creation of a fee simple determinable in the previous example) and the kind of language which states a condition subsequent (which resulted in the creation of a fee simple subject to a condition subsequent in this example) is very subtle indeed.

The fee simple subject to a condition subsequent is distinguished from the fee simple determinable in another way. In the example, if and when the land is no longer used for residential purposes, *O* has the power to end *A*'s estate by entering the land or by otherwise indicating his desire to retake possession. But *A*'s estate does not end automatically, as in the case of a fee simple determinable.

[D] Fee simple subject to an executory limitation (fee simple subject to an executory interest)

Finally, the transferor can attach a condition subsequent to a fee simple, as in the previous example, but provide that a second transferee, instead of the transferor himself, is entitled to possession when the condition is met.

> **Example 2-5**
> *O* conveys "to *A*, but if the land is not used for residential purposes during *A*'s lifetime, to *B*."

As in the previous example, the "but if" clause states a condition subsequent, and we *could* say that *A* has a fee simple subject to a condition subsequent. That term, however, implies that *A*'s interest is followed by an interest in the *transferor* (a right of entry). Instead, we usually say that *A* has a fee simple subject to an executory limitation (also called a fee simple subject to an executory interest). That term indicates that *A*'s interest is followed by an interest in another *transferee*. (The "but if" clause here is an executory limitation, which is really just one kind of condition subsequent. *B* has a shifting executory interest.)

A transferor could also create a fee simple determinable in *A* followed by an executory interest in *B*. See § 3.08[C][1].

The fee simple conditional and fee tail are two other kinds of fee estates. They are obsolete almost everywhere, however, and we shall not discuss them or use them in examples.

[E] Life estate

If a transferee has the right of possession until he dies, he has a life estate.

Example 2-6
O conveys "to *A* for life."

A has a life estate. (If *A* had been given the right of possession until the death of some other person, *A* would have a life estate "pur autre vie"--"for another life.")

[F] Leaseholds

The transferee may be given the right of possession for a specified number of years, months, or shorter periods of time (an estate for years or a term of years), a similar period of time which renews automatically unless one party gives notice (a periodic tenancy), or as long as both parties desire the tenancy to continue (a tenancy at will).

§ 2.03 Future interests in the transferor (reversionary interests)

If there is the certainty or possibility that the right of possession will return to the transferor in the future, he has retained a future interest.

[A] Possibility of reverter

The possibility that a transferor will regain the right of possession after the termination of a fee simple determinable is called a possibility of reverter. In Example 2-3, § 2.02[B], *O* has a possibility of reverter.

[B] Right of entry

The possibility that a transferor will regain the right of possession after the termination of a fee simple subject to a condition subsequent (or after the termination of some other estate which is subject to a condition subsequent) is called a right of entry. In Example 2-4, § 2.02[C], *O* has a right of entry.

Other names for the right of entry are right of re-entry, right of (re-)entry for condition broken, right of entry for breach of condition, and power of termination.

[C] Reversion

If there exists the certainty or possibility that the right of possession will return to *O*, and *O*'s interest fits neither the definition of a possibility of reverter nor the definition of a right of entry, then it is a reversion. Of course, there exists a more formal definition, but this one is sufficient for our purposes.

Example 2-7
O conveys to *A* for life.

O has not stated who is entitled to possession when *A* dies, so *O* himself must have retained the right of possession when that occurs. *O* has a reversion.

Example 2-8
O conveys to *A* for life, then to *B* if *B* survives *A*.

Here, *O* has not stated who is entitled to possession in case *B* does not survive *A*. Therefore, the right of possession must return to *O* under those circumstances, and *O* has retained a reversion. Unlike the reversion in Example 2-7, the reversion here represents only the *possibility* that *O* will regain the right of possession.

§ 2.04 Future interests in a transferee

It is customary to divide the future interests in transferees into two groups: remainders and executory interests. Remainders, in turn, are divided into contingent remainders and vested remainders, and vested remainders are subdivided into three types. Executory interests, which are almost always contingent, are sometimes divided into those that are "springing" and those that are "shifting." Thus, the usual classification scheme is as follows:

> Remainders
>> Contingent
>> Vested
>>> Absolutely vested
>>> Vested subject to partial divestment
>>> Vested subject to complete divestment
>
> Executory interests
>> Springing
>> Shifting

This scheme is not particularly useful when discussing the Rule against Perpetuities. The basis for distinguishing between the remainder and the executory interest is historical, and the differences in legal result between those two interests have largely disappeared. In particular, the Rule applies in the same way to both the remainder and the executory interest,[1] so no attempt will be made to draw a formal distinction between the two. For purposes of applying the Rule, what *is* important is the distinction between interests which are vested and those which are contingent. That distinction requires an understanding, in turn, of the difference between a "condition precedent" and a "condition subsequent." In order to make our review of future interests most useful for an understanding of the Rule against Perpetuities, our discussion will be organized as follows:

---

[1] But if the doctrine of destructibility of contingent remainders is still in force (and it is *not* in force in almost all states), a proper application of the Rule may depend on the proper classification of an interest as a remainder or an executory interest. See § 6.05.

1. The difference between a condition precedent and a condition subsequent
2. Contingent interests
3. Vested interests
   (a) Absolutely vested
   (b) Vested subject to partial divestment
   (c) Vested subject to complete divestment

[A] The difference between a condition precedent and a condition subsequent

Earlier we made the distinction between a "condition subsequent" and a "special limitation." In this section, we make the distinction between a "condition subsequent" and a "condition precedent."

An interest is said to be subject to a *condition precedent* if, when a specified condition is satisfied, the owner of the interest is *entitled* to possession of the underlying property. (He may, however, also have to wait for the termination of the preceding estate(s).)

An interest is said to be subject to a *condition subsequent* if, when a specified condition is satisfied, the owner of the interest is *denied* the right of possession of the underlying property, and the right of present or future possession passes to someone else. (As we have seen, however, the phrases "for so long as," "until," and the like state a "special limitation," not a condition subsequent. See § 2.02[B].) We use "condition subsequent" here to include an executory limitation (see § 2.02[D]).

Example 2-9
To *A* for life, then to *B* if *B* survives *A*.

B's interest is subject to a condition precedent. The words "if *B* survives *A*" state the condition precedent.

Example 2-10
To *A* if he marries.

A's interest is subject to a condition precedent, stated by the words "if he marries."

Example 2-11
To *A* for life, then to *B* if he marries.

Again, *B*'s interest is subject to a condition precedent. Here, satisfaction of the condition precedent does not mean that *B* will be entitled to possession immediately; he still has to wait for *A*'s life estate to end.

Example 2-12
To *A* for life, then to *B*, but if *B* dies without issue surviving him, to *C*.

If the condition is satisfied (that is, if *B* dies without issue surviving him), *C* will be entitled to possession. (If *A* is still alive, *C* will have to wait for *A*'s estate to end first.) Therefore, we can say that *C*'s interest is subject to a *condition precedent*.

What we have said does not completely describe the effect of satisfying the condition, however. If *B* dies without issue surviving him, *B* will be *denied* possession of the property. Referring to the definition of "condition subsequent" given above, we would say that *B*'s interest is subject to a *condition subsequent* (more precisely, an executory limitation). You can see, then, that the condition "but if *B* dies without issue surviving him" does double duty. It makes *C*'s interest subject to a condition precedent, *and* it makes *B*'s interest subject to a condition subsequent. What, then, shall we call the condition: precedent or subsequent? We *could* call it both, but we usually use the label "condition subsequent" and let it go at that. By definition, *every* condition subsequent entitles one person to possession while denying another person possession; a condition subsequent will always act in the double-ended character illustrated by this example. If a particular condition is described as a "condition subsequent," everyone understands that it actually acts both as a condition subsequent (with respect to the preceding interest) and as a condition precedent (with respect to the succeeding interest).

[B] Contingent interests

An interest is contingent if:
(a) it is subject to some condition precedent, *or*
(b) it is given to a person who is unborn or unascertained.

An interest may be *both* subject to a condition precedent *and* given to an unborn or unascertained person. You can see that "contingent" has a broader meaning than "subject to a condition precedent."

There are two kinds of contingent interests: contingent remainders and contingent executory interests. (Almost every executory interest is contingent, so we usually omit the label "contingent" when referring to executory interests.) We will not be explaining the difference between them, however, because the Rule applies in the same way to both.[2]

Point of potential confusion:
Disagreement about terminology

There is considerable disagreement about the precise meaning of the terms we are using to describe a contingent remainder. Some other meanings are given below, in order to prevent confusion if you should see these terms used in a slightly

---

[2]However, if the doctrine of destructibility of contingent remainders is in force, a proper application of the Rule may depend on the classification of the interest as a contingent remainder or executory interest. See § 6.05.

different way in your other reading.

1. Some authorities use the term "condition precedent" to include the requirement that the preceding estate end before the owner of the future interest is entitled to possession or enjoyment.[3]   Under this definition, even vested (non-contingent) future interests are subject to a condition precedent, because even vested estates are subject to the requirement that the preceding estate must end. Because this "requirement" is not very important in applying the Rule, for our purposes the narrower definition we have given is preferable.

2. Some authors use the term "condition precedent" to include the requirement that a person be born or ascertained.

3. Sometimes the term "unascertained person" is used to include unborn persons. However, using two mutually exclusive terms, as we do, is useful because they help to emphasize the various ways in which an interest can be contingent.

Below we give examples of contingent interests.

Example 2-13
To *A* for life, then to *B* if *B* survives *A*.

The requirement that *B* survive *A* is a condition precedent. *B* has a contingent interest. (It is a contingent remainder. A common way of stating the same conveyance is "to *A* for life, *remainder* to *B* if *B* survives *A*.")

Example 2-14
To *A* for life, then to *A*'s first child.

Facts: *A* has not had any children.

A's first child is unborn. Therefore, there is a contingent interest in *A*'s first child. (It is a contingent remainder.) While it seems odd to say that there is an interest in a nonexistent person, that is the customary way of describing the state of the title in a conveyance like this one.

Example 2-15
To *A* for life, then to *A*'s widow.

---

[3]For example, Gray says that a remainder is vested if there is no condition precedent "other than the natural termination of the preceding estate." Gray, Rule against Perpetuities, § 101 (4th ed. 1942).

Note that *A*'s widow is simply the person to whom *A* is married at his death. We do not know who that person will be (if anyone). Therefore, *A*'s widow has a contingent interest because she is unascertained. (Note that even if *A* has a wife now, the marriage could end by divorce or the wife's death, and *A* could remarry. Then someone else would be *A*'s widow at his death.)[4]

Example 2-16
To *A* if *A* has a child.

Facts: *A* has not had any children.

The requirement that *A* have a child is a condition precedent, and *A* has a contingent interest. (It is a springing executory interest.)

Example 2-17
To *A* for life, then to *B*, but if *B* dies without issue surviving him, to *C*.

The condition "but if *B* dies without issue surviving him," is a condition precedent with respect to *C*'s interest (see § 2.04[A]). Therefore, *C* has a contingent interest (it is a shifting executory interest).

Example 2-18
To *A* for life, then to *B* for life, then to *C*.

B's interest, being a life estate, lasts only as long as he remains alive. Therefore, if *B* dies before *A* dies, neither *B* nor his succesors will be entitled to possession. Is there a condition precedent, then, that *B* survive *A*? The answer is no. The "requirement" that *B* be alive at *A*'s death is inherent in the nature of *B*'s interest (a life estate) rather than the result of a condition precedent to which his interest is subject. *B*'s interest is *not* contingent. (*B*'s interest is described in Example 2-23, § 2.04[C][3].)

[C] Vested interests

An interest is vested if it is not contingent.[5] Referring to the definition of contingent interest given above, we can say that an interest is vested if it is not subject to any condition precedent and it is given to a born and ascertained person.[6] There is

---

[4]Because of the strong preference for vested interests, it is possible that in a particular case the court would construe the interest as vested subject to divestment by the death or divorce of *A*'s present wife.

[5]Note, however, the exception for some kinds of executory interests (§ 3.08[B]).

[6]Some courts use "vested" to mean "not subject to a condition of survivorship," but that usage is simply the result of carelessness.

a more formal, technical definition, but for our purposes this one is sufficient.

All vested future interests in transferees are remainders.[7] In the discussion that follows, therefore, we shall be speaking of "vested remainders" instead of "vested interests."

A present estate will always be vested.

There are three kinds of vested remainders: absolutely vested, vested subject to partial divestment, and vested subject to complete divestment.

[1] Absolutely vested

> **Example 2-19**
> To *A* for life, then to *B*.

B's interest is a vested remainder. The simplest route to that conclusion is simply to note the absence of any reason for labeling it contingent. First, there is no condition precedent. In particular, the fact that *B*'s right of possession is postponed until *A* dies is not a "condition precedent." (But see the "Point of potential confusion" in § 2.04[B].) Note that, if *B* dies during *A*'s lifetime, then *B*'s heirs or will beneficiaries succeed to *B*'s interest. Later, when *A* dies, *B*'s heirs or will beneficiaries (as the case may be) will be entitled to possession. That result should make clear to you that there is no condition precedent that *B* survive *A*. The owner of the remainder-- whether he be *B* or someone else--will be entitled to possession when *A* dies, regardless of whether *B* survived *A* or not.

Second, *B* is a living person; he is not "unborn." (Throughout this book, we assume that a person identified with a letter is an actual living person.)

Third, *B* is not unascertained. It is true, as we just explained, that we do not know the identity of the person who will actually be entitled to possession after *A*'s death: he might be *B* or he might be an heir or will beneficiary of *B*. Indeed, he might be someone to whom *B* transferred his interest during his lifetime. But this uncertainty does not make the owner of the remainder an "unascertained" person. At every moment from the time of the conveyance until the life estate ends, we will be able to point to some real person and say about him, "This is the person who would be entitled to possession if *A* were to die now." It is our ability always to point to the present owner of the interest that enables us to say that the interest is given to an ascertained person.

B's remainder is *absolutely* vested because it will not be cut short or made "smaller" in any way, as is the case with the other two kinds of vested remainder.[8]

---

[7]Some executory interests, however, are treated under the Rule *as if* they were vested (§ 3.08[B]).

[8]The Restatement's term "indefeasibly vested" has approximately the same meaning as "absolutely vested." 2 Restatement of Property § 157 (1936).

Vested with postponed enjoyment

In some cases, a condition which appears to require that a transferee survive until a certain time is interpreted instead merely to postpone the time for possession or payment. The interest is vested.

Example 2-20
T makes a bequest of $1000 "to A, to be paid at age 25."

The "to be paid" language is interpreted to postpone the time for payment until A reaches 25 but not to require that A actually live to be 25; A's interest is vested.[9] Because there is no condition of survivorship, A's interest passes to his heirs or will beneficiaries if he dies before reaching 25. Then they are entitled to payment at the time when A *would have* reached 25 had he lived. No distribution is made to A's heirs or will beneficiaries immediately upon A's death before reaching 25 because to do so would prematurely terminate the interest of whoever is entitled to receive the *income* from the $1000 pending distribution. If that income beneficiary is A himself, there is no objection to paying the $1000 to A's heirs or will beneficiaries immediately upon A's death.[10]

[2] Vested subject to partial divestment

Example 2-21
To A for life, then to A's children.

Facts: A has one child, $C1$.

$C1$ has a vested remainder: there is no condition precedent, and $C1$ is born and ascertained.

However, as long as A is alive, A can have more children. As more children are born, they all share in the remainder, and $C1$'s interest becomes smaller. This process of cutting down $C1$'s interest is called "partial divestment," and $C1$'s interest is said to be "vested subject to partial divestment."[11] As each new child is born, he too acquires a remainder which is vested subject to partial divestment.

Sometimes it is said that an interest which is vested subject to partial divestment is not "vested" for purposes of the Rule. This statement is an attempt to describe how the Rule applies to class gifts, but it is more confusing than helpful.

---

[9] It is not, however, a remainder. An equivalent interest in land would be called an executory interest (actually, an executory devise, since it is by will).

[10] L. Simes and A. Smith, The Law of Future Interests § 589 (2d ed. 1956).

[11] The Restatement uses the term "vested subject to open." 2 Restatement of Property § 157 (1936).

The unborn children have a contingent interest, precisely because they are unborn. Although by "long established usage" the unborn children are thought to take as remaindermen,[12] some authors consider the unborn children to take by way of executory interest,[13] and others say that the unborn children's interest is unique, classifiable neither as a contingent remainder nor as an executory interest.[14]

[3] Vested subject to complete divestment

An interest which is subject to a condition subsequent (including an executory limitation) is said to be "vested subject to complete divestment."[15]

> **Example 2-22**
> To A for life, then to B, but if B dies without issue surviving him, to C.

The condition "but if B dies without issue surviving him" is a condition subsequent *with respect to* B's interest (it is also an executory limitation; see § 2.02[D]). Therefore, B has a vested remainder subject to complete divestment.

> **Example 2-23**
> To A for life, then to B for life, then to C.

If B dies before A does, B will never be entitled to possession. The "requirement" that B outlive A is a result of the fact that B's interest is a life estate measured by his lifetime, rather than a fee or some other interest. B's interest is not subject to any condition subsequent. Therefore, B's interest is absolutely vested (it is an absolutely vested remainder for life).[16]

This example illustrates something important about the meaning of the term "remainder." That term says that a transferee, rather than the transferor, will be entitled to possession beginning at some future time (roughly, after one or more preceding less-than-fee estates have ended). But the term "remainder" does not specify *how long* the transferee will be entitled to possession. In Example 2-23, both B and C have remainders. Once A dies, B will be entitled to possession only for his own

---

[12] 1 American Law of Property § 4.34, at 465-466 (A. Casner ed. 1952).

[13] L. Waggoner, Future Interests in a Nutshell, § 6.3, at 70 (1981).

[14] L. Simes and A. Smith, The Law of Future Interests § 114 (2d ed. 1956).

[15] The Restatement's term of "vested subject to complete defeasance" has approximately the same meaning. 2 Restatement of Property § 157 (1936).

[16] The Restatement, however, would call B's interest "vested subject to complete defeasance." B's death before A results in the *defeasance* of B's interest (it ends) but not in its *divestment* (which would be caused by a condition subsequent). 2 Restatement of Property § 157, comment o, illustration 11 (1936).

lifetime, so he has a *"remainder for life."* *C*, on the other hand, will be entitled to possession forever, once *A* and *B* have died, so *C* has a *remainder in fee simple absolute.*

§ 2.05 Legal interests and equitable interests

Thus far we have been speaking mostly of legal interests in land. Today, most future interests are equitable interests in personalty, that is, interests created under a trust, in which all or most of the trust corpus consists of stocks, bonds, and other intangibles. But even in a trust, we speak of life estates, remainders, and reversions. Although some of the terms we have reviewed here are not usually used in connection with personal property, the concepts are the same.

Example 2-24
O conveys securities in trust, to pay the income to *A* for life, then to pay the income to *B* for life, then to pay the principal to *C*.

Here we would say that *A* has an equitable life estate and *B* has an equitable remainder for life. We would probably say simply that *C* has an equitable remainder; the term "fee" is not normally used in connection with personal property. If we do not further specify the kind of remainder that *C* has, the implication is that he will acquire absolute ownership of the trust property when *A* and *B* die; *C*'s interest is equivalent to a remainder in fee simple absolute in land.

The other concepts we have studied--conditions precedent and conditions subsequent, contingent and vested interests--generally apply to interests in personalty under a trust just as they apply to legal interests in land.[17]

§ 2.06 How a contingent interest can change

The Rule against Perpetuities is violated if--speaking very generally now--a contingent interest might remain in existence for too long. In order to apply the Rule, then, we must know how a contingent interest can lose its contingent character. That can happen in two ways. First, a contingent interest can change into a vested interest. Second, a contingent interest can disappear entirely, or "fail." In the paragraphs below we discuss how a contingent interest can vest or fail.

[A] A contingent interest can change into a vested interest

A contingent interest vests when the condition precedent (if any) is satisfied and when the transferee of the interest becomes born and ascertained (if that was not already the case). This, of course, is simply a restatement of the definition of a vested

---

[17]And, in this book we will use "heirs" to include those persons who succeed to an intestate's personal property as well as those persons who succeed to his real property.

interest.

Example 2-25
To *A* for life, then to *B* if *B* survives *A*.

B's interest will vest if he is alive at *A*'s death.

Example 2-26
To *A* for life, then to *B* if *B* marries.

B's interest will vest if he marries. In this example, *B*'s interest can vest before it becomes a present possessory interest (*i.e.*, before *A* dies).

Example 2-27
To *A* for life, then to *A*'s first child.

Facts: *A* has not had any children.

The interest in *A*'s first child will vest when the child is born.

Example 2-28
To *A* for life, then to *A*'s children.

Each unborn child's interest vests when he is born.

Example 2-29
To *A* for life, then to *A*'s widow.

The interest in *A*'s widow vests if *A* is married at his death.

[B] A contingent interest can fail

A contingent interest fails if there comes a time when the circumstances for it to become a present estate can *never* occur. To say that an interest "fails" is to say that it simply disappears; there is no reason to continue to recognize its existence once we know that it will never give its owner the right of possession of the land (or enjoyment of the trust fund). There are a number of ways, then, in which an interest might fail:

(a) If the interest is contingent because it is subject to a condition precedent, then the interest fails once the condition precedent becomes impossible to satisfy.

Example 2-30
To *A* for life, then to *B* if *B* survives *A*.

B's interest will fail if he dies while *A* is still alive.

Example 2-31
To *A* for life, then to *B* if *B* marries.

B's interest will fail if he dies without ever having married.

(b) If the interest is contingent because it is given to an unborn or un-ascertained person, then it fails if there comes a time when that person can never be born or ascertained.

Example 2-32
To *A* for life, then to *B*'s first child.

Facts: *B* has not had any children.

The interest in *B*'s first child will fail if *B* dies without having had any children.

Example 2-33
To *A* for life, then to *A*'s children.

The contingent interest in all potential (unborn) children of *A* fails when *A* dies.

(c) A contingent interest in potential (unborn) class members will fail when the class closes under the rule of convenience (as well as when it closes biologically, as in Example 2-33). (We discuss this in conjunction with class gifts, in Chapter 4.)

(d) A contingent interest may fail by virtue of the fact that it is less than a fee simple absolute. The most common example is a life estate: a life estate will fail at the death of the life tenant (or other person by whose lifetime the interest is measured, if it is a life estate pur autre vie) before the interest becomes possessory.

Example 2-34
To *A* for life, then to *B* for life if he has a child, then to *C*.

The interest in *B* will fail if *B* dies during *A*'s lifetime, even if *B* has had a child. (It will also fail, of course, if *B* dies without ever having had a child.)

(e) A power of appointment will fail (expire) when the donee dies, because powers are not devisable or inheritable. (A power of appointment is not a future interest, but we apply the Rule to it as if it were.) We discuss powers of appointment in Chapter .

(f) If the doctrine of destructibility of contingent remainders is still in force, a legal contingent interest in land fails if it has not vested by the time the preceding estate has ended. The doctrine is obsolete almost everywhere, so you will probably not have occasion to take this manner of failing into account. For more on the doctrine and an example, see § 6.05.

§ 2.07 Succession to future interests

What happens at the death of a person who owns one of the interests we have been discussing? Unless the interest fails at the owner's death, it will pass to the beneficiaries under his will or, if he has no will, to his heirs. In particular, contingent interests pass to the owner's will beneficiaries or heirs just as vested interests do, unless there is something about the contingent interest that requires the owner to survive longer. But, in general, we do not *imply* a condition of survivorship.

> **Example 2-35**
> To *A* for life, then to *B* for life.

Since *B*'s interest ends at his death, it will not pass to his will beneficiaries or heirs.

> **Example 2-36**
> To *A* for life, then to *B* if *B* survives *A*.

If *B* dies during *A*'s lifetime, *B*'s contingent remainder fails, so it will not pass to his will beneficiaries or heirs.

> **Example 2-37**
> To *A* for life, then to *B*.

If *B* dies during *A*'s lifetime, *B*'s remainder passes to his will beneficiaries or heirs.

> **Example 2-38**
> To *A* for life, then to *B* if *C* is admitted to the bar.

Assume that *B* dies during A's lifetime. Assume further that, at *B*'s death, *C* is alive and has not been admitted to the bar. Because *C* might still be admitted to the bar, *B*'s interest has not yet failed. Therefore, it will pass to his will beneficiaries or heirs.

Even in a gift to a class, a condition of survivorship is not ordinarily implied. (See § 4.01[B][2].)

Chapter 3
The basic operation of the Rule

___

In this chapter we learn how to apply the Rule to the simplest kind of future interest: one created in an individual. (In later chapters, we shall learn how the Rule applies to class gifts, powers of appointment, interests created under a power of appointment, and gifts in default of appointment.)

§ 3.01 First principles: what the Rule does

[A] Every future interest, with a few exceptions, must satisfy the Rule.

Almost every kind of future interest is subject to the Rule.[1] The Rule applies to personal property as well as real property, and equitable interests as well as legal interests. A few kinds of future interests, however, are not subject to the Rule; they are discussed in § 3.01[D].

If an interest does not satisfy the Rule, it is void (see § 3.01[C]).

Terminology
In order to be as general as possible, we shall usually use the word "transferor" to refer to the person who has created the future interests under discussion. It is useful to keep in mind, however, that most future interests today are created under a trust, and the "transferor" will usually be a testator who has created a testamentary trust or the settlor of an inter-vivos trust.

[B] The Rule applies to each interest, not to the instrument as a whole

The instrument which a transferor executes will often create several future interests. The Rule applies independently to each future interest. It is each future interest, and not the instrument as a whole, that must satisfy the Rule. If one interest is void under the Rule, it is very likely that other future interests created by the same instrument do satisfy the Rule.

Class gifts, however, are an exception to the principle that the Rule applies separately to each interest (see Chapter 4).

Sometimes, also, an interest will be void by "infectious invalidity." If this doctrine applies, the invalidity of one interest under the Rule causes the court to strike one or more other interests in the same instrument. The basis for holding the other interests void is the transferor's presumed intent, however, rather than the Rule itself.

___

[1]Contingent easements and profits a prendre are also subject to the Rule, though real covenants and equitable servitudes are not. L. Simes and A. Smith, The Law of Future Interests § 1246, at 165 and § 1248, at 168-169 (2d ed. 1956).

(The doctrine is discussed in § 6.01.)

[C] If an interest does not satisfy the Rule, it is a complete nullity

An interest which does not satisfy the Rule is void, a complete nullity--almost as if the words which purported to create it had never been written. It is not correct, then, to say that an interest that does not satisfy the Rule "becomes" void some time after it was created (for example, when a court decides that the Rule has been violated). Rather, the "interest" was void from the moment the transferor attempted to create it, and it never really existed at all.

For convenience, we shall continue to use the word "interest" to refer to something that, because it violates the Rule, does not actually exist. We shall use the terms "void," "invalid," and "bad" interchangeably to describe an interest which violates the Rule. Similarly, the terms "valid" and "good" describe an interest which satisfies the Rule.

The invalidity of an interest under the Rule usually means that the transferor has not made a complete disposition of the property. Therefore, he will have retained a future interest (usually a reversion). (For an example where the invalidity of an interest does *not* result in an incomplete disposition of the transferor's property, see § 3.08[C][1].)

[D] Interests which are not subject to the Rule

Some interests are not subject to the Rule; they are discussed in the following paragraphs.

[1] Reversionary interests are not subject to the Rule

The reversion, the possibility of reverter, and the right of entry are not subject to the Rule. Thus, except for options (§ 6.02), interests retained by or created in the transferor are not subject to the Rule. (Naturally, it makes no difference whether we say that these interests are "not subject" to the Rule or that they are "always valid" under the Rule. You might come across the second description elsewhere in your reading.)

Alternatively, we can say that the reversion is valid under the Rule because it is a vested interest, and vested interests are not subject to the Rule (see § 3.01[D][4]). Sometimes it is said that the possibility of reverter and the right of entry are "vested" for purposes of the Rule. That is simply another way of saying that the Rule does not apply to them.

[2] An interest that is subject to a power in one person to make himself the absolute owner of the property is not subject to the Rule

Suppose that the transferor has created several future interests in Blackacre, but he has retained the power to make himself the absolute owner of Blackacre once again (*i.e.*, to create in himself the present possessory fee simple absolute in Blackacre). So tenuous is the existence of the future interests that we treat them as if they did not exist. This principle has been stated: "So long as one person has an unrestricted present power to alienate absolutely and in fee simple for his own benefit no future interest can be void" under the Rule against Perpetuities.[2]

This principle is most commonly applied when a transferor creates a revocable trust. If the transferor were to revoke the trust, he would become absolute owner of the trust corpus, terminating the trust and destroying all the future interests in the trust beneficiaries. Therefore, future interests under a revocable trust are not subject to the Rule as long as the trust remains revocable. A settlor's unlimited power to consume the principal of the trust is equivalent to a power of revocation.

The way in which the Rule applies to a general power of appointment exercisable by deed or will also reflects the principle we have been discussing, but we leave the details to § 5.03.

Important: We have said that the Rule does not apply to a future interest that is subject to a power in one person to make himself the absolute owner, but we do not mean that the Rule will *never* apply to such an interest. Once the interest can no longer be destroyed by exercise of that power, the principle discussed in this section no longer applies. So, for example, when a revocable trust becomes irrevocable (usually at the death of the settlor), the Rule *then* applies to the future interests under the trust. The consequences of postponing the application of the Rule in this way are explored in § 3.03[B].

[3] An interest in a charity, following an interest in another charity, is not subject to the Rule

> **Example 3-1**
> *O* conveys "to the American Cancer Society, provided that, if a cure for cancer is found, then to the Society for the Prevention of Blindness."

If it were not for the exception now under discussion, the future interest in the Society for the Prevention of Blindness would be subject to the Rule. However, since both the present interest (in the American Cancer Society) and the future interest are created in charities, the Rule does not apply. Similarly, the Rule would not apply if the transferees were the trustees of trusts for charitable purposes instead of the charitable corporations themselves.

[4] Vested interests are not subject to the Rule

Vested interests are not subject to the Rule. (We might give the equivalent statement that vested interests are always valid under the Rule.)

---

[2] L. Simes and A. Smith, The Law of Future Interests § 1250, at 172 (2d ed. 1956).

Point of potential confusion

The Rule applies only to future interests. To say that present interests are not subject to the Rule is not to say that all present interests are unaffected by the Rule. If a present interest is subject to divestment by an executory interest, but the executory interest is invalid under the Rule, then the present interest will be "enlarged" from a vested interest subject to complete divestment to an absolutely vested interest. See § 3.08[C][1].

---

§ 3.02 The essence of the Rule

Reduced to its most basic form, the Rule can be stated as follows:

An interest is invalid if there is any possibility, no matter how unlikely, that the interest might remain contingent for longer than the maximum period allowed under the Rule.

This statement describes when an interest is *invalid* under the Rule. Another way of stating the Rule is to describe when an interest is *valid*:

An interest is valid if it is certain to either vest or fail no later than the end of the maximum period allowed under the Rule.

Recall that the two ways in which a contingent interest will *not* remain contingent are (1) changing into a vested interest and (2) failing (disappearing completely) (§ 2.06). You can see, then, that the two descriptions of the Rule given above are equivalent.

You can see also why we said earlier that all vested interests are valid under the Rule. Any interest which is not now contingent will obviously not remain contingent beyond the maximum allowable time.

The maximum period allowed under the Rule is called the "perpetuities period." Our discussion of the *length* of the perpetuities period will be given in a later section. For now, we will discuss exactly *what it is that must occur within the period.*

§ 3.03 What it means to say that there must be no possibility of an interest remaining contingent beyond the perpetuities period

[A] In general

An interest is either valid or invalid under the Rule *at the time the interest is (purportedly) created.* It is not accurate to say that an interest "becomes" invalid under the Rule when a court decides that the interest violates the Rule. Rather, a court "discovers" that the interest was invalid from the start (and therefore the purported "interest" never existed at all). For convenience, however, we will continue to refer to the time when an interest was "created" even though we may conclude that the interest is invalid and, therefore, never really created at all.

For this reason, it is also wrong to say that the Rule is satisfied if the interest we are considering *actually* ceases being contingent within the perpetuities period. The Rule is satisfied only if, *viewing the interest at the moment it was created*, we can show that there was *then* no possibility that the interest would still be contingent at the end of the perpetuities period. The requirement that we view the interest from the moment of its creation means that, in determining whether there was any possibility that the interest might remain contingent for too long a time, we are allowed to *take into account only those facts which existed at the time the interest was created.* Only the facts existing then can be considered because it was then that the interest was either valid or invalid. In short, the Rule is concerned with what *might* have happened (and what *might* still happen), not what *does* happen.

[B] Exception: Revocable interests

In § 3.01[D][2], we noted that the Rule does not apply to a revocable interest until it becomes irrevocable. That result can be restated in terms of an exception to the principle of this section.

The relevant time for evaluating the validity of an interest under *a revocable trust* is the moment *when it first becomes irrevocable* (usually at the death of the settlor). Therefore, the Rule is satisfied for interests under a revocable interest only if, *viewing the interest at the moment the trust became irrevocable,* we can show that there was *then* no possibility that the interest would still be contingent at the end of the perpetuities period. This means that, in determining whether there was any possibility that the interest under a revocable trust might remain contingent for too long a time, we are allowed to *take into account only those facts which existed at the time the trust became irrevocable.*[3] (We shall see later that another way of expressing the same concept is to say that the perpetuities period does not "start" until the trust becomes irrevocable.)

In the remainder of this book, then, a reference to the time when an interest was "created" or when an instrument "took effect" should be understood to refer--if we are dealing with a revocable interest--to the time when the interest became irrevocable.

[C] Illustrating the "no-possibility" requirement

We can gain a better understanding of how the Rule works by considering the following example.

---

[3] A revocable *legal* interest, of course, would receive similar treatment. Moreover, we shall see that a similar principle is applied in connection with a general power of appointment exercisable by deed or will. See § 5.03.

Example 3-2
O conveys Blackacre "to *A*, but if someone climbs the Sears Tower in Chicago, to *B*."

B's interest is contingent, because *B* is entitled to possession only if the condition (someone climbing the Sears Tower) is satisfied. (We assume, of course, that the Tower has not yet been climbed.) Although we haven't stated how long the perpetuities period is, let us assume that, at least, it is not *indefinitely* long. Knowing that, we can conclude that *B*'s interest is invalid under the Rule. The reasoning is as follows. *B*'s interest will *fail* if and when there is no longer any possibility that someone will climb the Sears Tower, and that will be the case only when the Sears Tower is no longer standing. *B*'s interest will *vest*, on the other hand, when someone climbs it. We cannot know how long the Sears Tower will remain standing, nor can we know when (if ever) someone will climb it. Therefore, *B*'s interest could remain contingent indefinitely, and it is invalid under the Rule.

Point of potential confusion

Recall from our discussion earlier (§ 2.07) that *B*'s interest, because it is not subject to any condition of survivorship, will pass upon his death to his heirs or will beneficiaries. It should be clear, then, that *B*'s interest can remain contingent beyond his lifetime.

Suppose that, one day after the conveyance, someone climbs the Sears Tower, and the following day *B* brings an action to eject *A* from Blackacre. *B* argues that his interest is valid under the Rule and that he is now entitled to possession. His interest vested one day after the conveyance, *B*'s argument goes, so his interest did not *actually* remain contingent beyond the perpetuities period. (Again, we have not discussed the actual length of the perpetuities period, but let us assume that it is longer than one or two days.) *B's argument is wrong.* *B*'s interest is invalid under the Rule, and he is not entitled to possession. It is irrelevant that *B*'s interest *did* vest within the perpetuities period. *B*'s interest *might not* have vested within the perpetuities period, *in light of the facts existing at the time the interest was created*, that is, before the Sears Tower was climbed. Even though we are actually evaluating the validity of the interest at some time after its creation, we must pretend that we are doing so at the moment of its creation, using only the facts that were known (or could have been known) at that time.

Because *B*'s interest is invalid, *A* has a present estate in fee simple absolute. We must recognize that the only way in which *A*'s estate might have been cut short was by *B*'s estate becoming a present one. But *B*'s interest does not, in fact, exist--that is the meaning of our conclusion that it is invalid under the Rule. Therefore, *A*'s estate will not be cut short by *B*'s interest and will instead last forever: *A*'s estate is a fee simple absolute. Declaring *B*'s interest invalid is like taking a pen to the instrument and striking the language which purported to create his interest. In doing so, we strike the words of condition, "but if someone climbs the Sears Tower," as well as the words "to *B*." We are left only with the words "to *A*," which create a fee simple absolute in *A*. (For further discussion of this topic, see § 3.08[C][1].)

Point of potential confusion

Recall that we said above that an interest is *valid* under the Rule if we are certain that it will either vest or *fail* within the perpetuities period. Sometimes a student will say something like this: "What sense does it make to say that if an interest *fails* within the perpetuities period, then it is *valid* under the Rule? What good does it do to prove the validity of an interest under the Rule if it is going to fail anyway?"

Those remarks reflect a misunderstanding of what the Rule requires. Once we have proved an interest is valid under the Rule, we still do not know *which* of the two, vesting or failing, is going to happen within the perpetuities period. We only know that *one or the other* will happen, because that is all the Rule requires us to prove. The owner of a valid contingent future interest can only hope that the interest turns out to vest rather than to fail. If, on the other hand, an interest were invalid under the Rule, then the "owner" of that interest would have no chance at all of enjoying the property, because the interest would not exist at all.

---

§ 3.04 The perpetuities period

We have spoken of a "perpetuities period" under the Rule. In this section we finally discuss the length (and nature) of this period. Surprisingly, we shall see that the perpetuities "period" is a real period of time only in a very unconventional sense.

The length of the perpetuities period is the lifetime of an actual person who was alive at the time the interest was created, followed by an additional 21 years.

Describing the period in a slightly different--but equivalent--way, we can say that the "deadline" for vesting or failing is *21 years after the death of some actual person who was alive at the time the interest was created.*

The *beginning* of the perpetuities period--when it "starts"--is when the interest under consideration was created, and that will be when the deed, will, or other instrument took effect. A will, of course, does not take effect until the testator dies. In the case of an interest under a revocable trust, we learned that the Rule does not apply until the trust becomes irrevocable (§ 3.01[D][2]). We can express that concept in a slightly different way by saying that, *for an interest under a revocable trust, the perpetuities period starts when the trust becomes irrevocable*, usually at the death of the settlor.

Terminology

The following terms will be used frequently in the remainder of this book. It is important that you memorize their meanings now.

1. The person whose lifetime is used to measure the perpetuities period is called, naturally enough, the *measuring life.*

2. A person who was alive when the interest was created (and who may or may not be the measuring life) is said to be *"in being"*--short for "in being at the time the interest was created."

Point of potential confusion

In your other reading you may see the term "life in being." That term will be avoided here because of its potential ambiguity. It could mean either one of the following:

(1) The actual person whose lifetime is used to measure the perpetuities period. This usage probably derives from Gray's description of the perpetuities period as "twenty-one years after some life in being at the creation of the interest." We (and most others) will call this person the "measuring life" instead.

(2) *Any* person who was in existence when the interest was created. We shall use the term "in being" or "person in being" to describe such a person, but we shall not use the term "life in being."

Although we have described the perpetuities period as the lifetime of a particular person (the "measuring life") followed by another 21 years, the perpetuities period may not actually include the *entire* lifetime of the measuring life. Because the perpetuities period does not "start" until the interest is created, which might be some time after the birth of the measuring life, the period might more accurately be described as *that portion* of the measuring life's lifetime which occurs after the interest is created, plus another 21 years.

The perpetuities period might be illustrated as in the diagram below. (It is not to scale.)

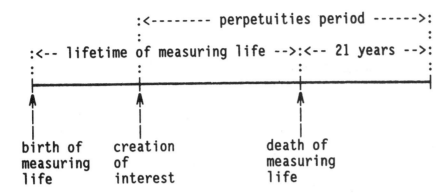

We must qualify our description of the perpetuities period in two ways:

[1] A person who has been conceived but not yet born can be a measuring life

We have said that the person who is the measuring life need only be alive at the very moment when the interest was created.   The period of time, shown in the diagram above, between the birth of the measuring life and the creation of the interest might be very short.   Moreover, for purposes of the Rule--as for most purposes in property law--a person who has been conceived but not yet born is treated in the same way as a person who has been born.   Therefore, a person who had only been conceived at the time the interest was created can serve as the measuring life.   For convenience, we have labeled one of the points in the diagram above as the *birth* of the measuring life, but in some circumstances that point would actually mark the *conception* of the measuring life, and his birth would occur after the interest was created.

[2] The perpetuities period is extended by actual periods of gestation

The second qualification about our description of the perpetuities period is stated here for the sake of completeness, even though its meaning will not be clear until later (see, *e.g.*, Example 3-9, § 3.07).   The perpetuities period is *extended* by any actual period of gestation, the period of time between a person's conception and his birth.

The odd thing about the Rule is that it does not appear to identify the measuring life, this person who was alive when the interest was created.   How, then, do we know who he is, so that we may know the length of the perpetuities period?   Although it is true that the Rule does not *directly* identify this person, the Rule does so *indirectly*.

To see what we mean, recall what we have already learned about the Rule. If we wish to prove that a particular interest is valid under the Rule, then we must prove that there is no possibility that the interest might still be contingent 21 years after the death of some person (the measuring life) who was alive when the interest was created. *It is the task of the lawyer who is trying to prove that the interest is valid to find an actual person who can be used as the measuring life.* Identifying the person who qualifies as the measuring life is part of the proof that an interest is valid under the Rule. Indeed, it is the central part of that proof. We explore these ideas further in the next section.

§ 3.05 The meaning of the measuring life

Up to this point, we have described the Rule in two ways. First, we said that an interest is valid under the Rule if, viewed from the time of its creation, it will surely vest or fail within the perpetuities period. Second, we have defined the perpetuities period as the lifetime of a "measuring life" (someone in existence at the creation of the interest) plus 21 years. We can now combine those two concepts by describing *when an interest is valid, or invalid, in terms of the measuring life.*

[A] When an interest is valid

An interest is valid if, at the time the interest was created, there existed an actual person about whom we could have said: "We know that 21 years after this person's death, this interest will not still be contingent, because it will have either vested or failed."

In other words, an interest is valid if there existed a person who will "work" as a measuring life. The way to prove the validity of the interest is to identify that person.

Recall that the only facts which we are allowed to take into account are facts existing at the time the interest was created. One fact which we *cannot* take into account, then, is how long our measuring life actually lived.

Perhaps you can see now why we said earlier that the perpetuities "period" is not a normal period of time. The Rule does not describe one fixed period applicable to all interests. Instead, the perpetuities period represents an entire *class* of periods, which are alike only in that each of them is measured by the lifetime of some person followed by an additional 21 years. Every future interest which is valid will have its *own* measuring life and, in a sense, its own perpetuities period (although the same person can serve as the measuring life for more than one interest). Moreover, even after we have selected a measuring life, still we have not completely fixed the length of the perpetuities period, because we do not know how long that person will live. We shall see later that, despite this daunting uncertainty, we *can* prove that an interest (if it is valid) will vest or fail no later than 21 years after the death of an appropriately chosen person.

The process of proving an interest valid by finding a measuring life can be illustrated by an example. Suppose that you have succeeded in proving that your client's interest (which he received under *T*'s will) will surely vest or fail no later than 21 years after the death of *T*'s son, but you cannot prove that that will happen within 21 years of the death of *T*'s widow. (How one can actually make such a proof will be discussed shortly.) Assume also that *T*'s son was "in being" at the time your client's interest was created (obviously, *T*'s son was either born or conceived before *T*'s death). In that case, your client's interest is good. The fact that *T*'s son can be identified as a person who will "work" as the "measuring life" is sufficient to establish the validity of the interest. It is entirely irrelevant that there is someone *else* (*T*'s widow in this hypothetical case) who will *not* work as a measuring life. In many cases, there will be one person who will work as a measuring life and billions of other persons (*i.e.*, everyone else on earth) who will not work.

[B] When an interest is invalid

An interest is invalid if, at the time the interest was created, there did *not* exist any person about whom we could have said: "We know that 21 years after this person's death, this interest will not still be contingent."

To establish the invalidity of an interest, then, it is necessary to prove that it is *impossible to find a person who qualifies as a measuring life.*

You can see, then, that it is wrong to speak of a measuring life for an interest which is invalid; the interest is invalid precisely because no measuring life can be found. In fact, it might be said that there is not even a "perpetuities period" for an invalid interest. (Nevertheless, some courts persist in confusing us by referring to a "measuring life" even when the interest is invalid.)

An example can be used to illustrate what we have been saying. Suppose that you *cannot* prove that your client's interest (which he received under *T*'s will) will surely vest or fail no later than 21 years after the death of *T*'s uncle. In other words, if you mentally place yourself at the time the interest was created, at *T*'s death, you can imagine one possible sequence of events which would result in the interest remaining contingent more than 21 years after the uncle's death. Therefore, the uncle will not work as a measuring life. But that is *not* sufficient to prove that your client's interest is invalid. The fact that the uncle will not work as a measuring life tells you nothing about whether or not there exists some *other* person who *will* work. Perhaps if you look harder you can find that other person, thereby proving the interest valid. On the other hand, perhaps you can prove that no other person works, thereby establishing the invalidity of the interest.

Let us return to the conveyance "to *A*, but if someone climbs the Sears Tower in Chicago, to *B*." We said before that *B*'s interest is invalid. Now we shall restate our conclusion in terms of the impossibility of finding a measuring life. As before, assume that someone climbed the Sears Tower one day after the conveyance was made, so that *B*'s interest--if it had been valid--would have vested at that time. Suppose further that we confirm that *B* was in existence when the conveyance was made and that he was still alive when his interest apparently vested. Can we say, then, that *B* works as a measuring life, since the interest actually vested within his lifetime (and therefore well within the lifetime-plus-21 years period)? The answer is no; *B* does not work as a measuring life. As we said previously, in proving that the interest must surely vest or fail within the period, we can take into account only those facts that were true when the interest was created. At that time, we could not have been certain that *B* would still be living when (if ever) the Sears Tower was climbed. The fact that a person whom we are considering as a measuring life was, in fact, still alive at a particular time *after the interest was created* is one of the facts which we *cannot* take into account. *B* does not work as a measuring life.

Nor is there anyone else who qualifies as a measuring life. We could select anyone in the world who was alive when the conveyance was made, repeat the above discussion using *his* name instead of *B*'s, and conclude that that person does not work as a measuring life either. Since it is impossible to find a person who will work as a measuring life, *B*'s interest is invalid.

When we looked at this example previously (§ 3.03[C]), we explained that *B*'s interest is invalid because it could remain contingent indefinitely. We are simply expressing the same concept in a different way when we say that *B*'s interest is invalid because there is no measuring life.

§ 3.06 More on the measuring life

We note here several principles regarding the measuring life. You are not expected to fully understand them now, but we have gathered them in one place for the sake of convenience. Each of these principles will be explained and illustrated in an example later. After you have finished reading this chapter, you may want to return here for review.

[A] The Rule permits more than one measuring life

For convenience, we have been speaking of *one* measuring life. The Rule actually allows us to designate a *group* of persons as measuring lives. If we can prove that the interest must surely vest or fail not later than 21 years after *all* persons in our selected group have died, then the interest is good. In that case, we would say that the last surviving member of the group is the measuring life or, more commonly, that *all* the persons in the group are the measuring lives. It is *not* necessary to know which one of the persons in our group will live the longest.

In the remainder of this book, when we speak of "the measuring life," you should understand that to mean "the measuring life *or lives*."

The only restriction on naming a group of persons as the measuring lives is that the group must not be so large that ascertaining the time of death of the last surviving member would be unreasonably difficult (see Example 3-10, § 3.07[C]).

[B] The measuring life need not take an interest under the instrument or be mentioned in the instrument

Because the Rule allows anyone to be the measuring life, as long as he will "work," the measuring life need not be a transferee (see Example 3-4, § 3.07[C]) or even be mentioned in the instrument (see Example 3-13, § 3.07[C]).

[C] Different interests created by the same instrument need not (and usually do not) have the same measuring life

Because each interest is evaluated separately under the Rule (§ 3.01[B]), each interest can have its own measuring life.

[D] A person can qualify as a measuring life if he had been conceived when the interest was created, even if he had not yet been born

We have already noted this principle, but we repeat it here for convenience. A person who had been conceived when the interest was created is considered to have been in existence then. Therefore, he can serve as a measuring life (see Example 3-13, § 3.07[C]).

§ 3.07 How to find the measuring life or prove that none exists

Up to this point we have learned that an interest is valid under the Rule if there is a person who will work as a measuring life, and that an interest is invalid if there is no such person. The process of working with the Rule, then, involves finding a measuring life or proving that none exists. In this section we discuss how both of these are done.

[A] The principle of trying to find a measuring life[4]

In determining how long an interest might remain contingent, we cannot take into account any facts that occurred after the interest was created. That means we cannot take into account how long the interest *actually* remained contingent. Nor can we take into account the actual lifetime of any person who was "in being," that is, alive at the time the interest was created. How is it possible, then, to prove for *any* person in being that the interest necessarily must vest or fail within 21 years after his death, so that he can serve as a measuring life? *We can make that proof only for a person whose death causes the interest to vest or fail immediately or within another 21 years.*

Imagine a 21-year "timer" starting to count down at the death of the person who we *think* will work as a measuring life. In order for that person actually to *be* the measuring life, his death must cause the interest to either vest or fail, immediately or within another 21 years. Otherwise, when the timer "rings" at the expiration of the 21 years, the interest *might* still be contingent, and the person we have chosen will *not* have worked as the measuring life.

How do we go about finding a person whose death causes an interest to vest or fail, immediately or within another 21 years? Earlier, we listed the various kinds of events which would result in an interest vesting or failing. Obviously, then, we must find a person whose death brings about one of those events, either immediately or

---

[4]*See* Dukeminier, *Perpetuities: The Measuring Lives*, 85 Colum. L. Rev. 1648, 1650-1654 (1985).

within 21 years. (If you have not read the discussion regarding how an interest can vest or fail, you should read it now, in § 2.06.) If that person was "in being," we have found a measuring life, and the interest is good. (We have been speaking of *one* person who serves as the measuring life, but recall that the interest is good if we find a group of persons who will work as the measuring lives.)

Below we set out a four-step procedure for finding the measuring life (or proving that none can be found). The procedure implements the analysis in the preceding paragraphs. If you don't understand the four steps after reading them once or twice, don't dwell on them. Instead, move on to the examples that follow, where the procedure should become clearer as we apply it.

[B] Four steps to finding the measuring life or proving that none exists

Step 1. State the contingencies

By "contingencies," we mean *what must happen to cause the interest to vest.* Under step 1, then, we must identify the reasons the interest is contingent in the first place (conditions precedent, an unborn beneficiary, and/or an unascertained beneficiary) and then state those reasons in terms of requirements for vesting. For example, in "to A for life, then to B if living," the contingency is "B must be living at A's death," and in "to A for life, then to A's first child," the contingency is "A must have a child." Keep in mind that there may be more than one reason that the interest is contingent.

Perhaps you are saying to yourself that we should also state what must happen to cause the interest to *fail* (since the Rule requires either vesting or failing), but the most common way in which an interest fails is *implicit* in our statement of what must happen to cause the interest to vest. For example, if we state the contingency as "A must have a child," the interest will fail if A never has a child. (There are other ways in which an interest might fail, which are not implicit in our statement of the contingency, but we cover them as part of Step 2.)

Step 2: Find the "tentative measuring lives": all the persons whose deaths "resolve" one or more of the contingencies identified in Step 1, immediately or within 21 years.

When we say that someone's death "resolves" a contingency, we mean that his death either results in the contingency being satisfied (in which case the interest vests) or makes the contingency impossible to satisfy (in which case the interest fails). (We have seen that there are other ways in which an interest might fail (§ 2.06[B]), but we shall postpone consideration of them until later in Step 2.)

Therefore, if the interest is subject to a condition precedent, we must find someone whose death causes the condition to be satisfied or impossible to satisfy, immediately or within 21 years. If the interest is in an unborn/unascertained beneficiary, we must find someone whose death causes the beneficiary to be born/ascertained or prevents the beneficiary from being born/ascertained, immediately or within 21 years.

Note that there may be more than one contingency which must be resolved. One person may resolve all the contingencies, or we may have to find several persons who, together, resolve all the contingencies.

In this book, we shall call these persons the "tentative measuring lives." Although this term is not used elsewhere in perpetuities literature, it is useful here because it reminds us that we cannot know whether these persons will actually work as the measuring lives until we successfully complete Step 3.

Following are three useful facts to help us with Step 2. They are all very obvious, but there is some tendency to forget them in the stress of perpetuities analysis. Their usefulness will become clearer when we work some examples later, and you can review them at that time.

Fact #1: A contingency that a person must do something is resolved by the death of that person.

If the contingency is that a person must do something, then that person's death will resolve the contingency. Clearly he cannot do anything after he is dead. At his death, either he will have already taken the specified action (in which case the interest will have vested), or he will not have taken the specified action and can never do so (in which case the interest will have failed).

Requirements that a person must get married, or have a child, or be admitted to the bar are examples of the contingencies we are speaking of. Contingencies that a person be living at a specified time (a condition of survivorship) or that he reach a specified age are very common. These, too, can be satisfied only during the person's lifetime. Once he has died, either he will have already satisfied the contingency (*i.e.*, survived until a specified time or reached a specified age), or he will never do so. We should select the person himself as a tentative measuring life.

Fact #2: A contingency that a person must be born is resolved by the deaths of all his possible parents.

Very frequently, an interest is contingent for the reason that it is given to an unborn person. In such a case, the contingency is that the person must be born, and it will be resolved at the deaths of *all the possible parents* of that person. For example, the contingency that a child of *A* must be born will be resolved at *A*'s death. If *A* has not had a child by the time of his death, he will never have one. Therefore, for this contingency we would select *A* as the tentative measuring life under Step 2. It is true that *A* may, in fact, have a child after his death if *A* is male and his wife is pregnant at his death. But the actual measuring life may be someone who had only been conceived when the interest was created (§ 3.04), so we can say the same about our "tentative" measuring life.

As another example, the contingency of a *grandchild* of *A* being born will be resolved at the deaths of *all* of *A*'s children. If a grandchild has not been born by the time that all of *A*'s children have died, there will *never* be a grandchild. We would select "all of *A*'s children" as the tentative measuring lives under step 2.

Note the emphasis on *all* the possible parents as the tentative measuring lives. A possible parent might be someone who has not yet been born at the creation of the interest. For example, suppose we have identified the contingency as "a grandchild of

A must be born," and A has one child, C1, at the time the interest was created. The contingency will be resolved at the deaths of *all the possible parents* of the unborn grandchild, and all the possible parents are *all* of A's children, including C1 and *any children that* A *might have later* (see Example 3-12, § 3.07[C]).

Fact #3: A contingency that a person must reach age X *will be resolved within* X *years of the deaths of all his possible parents.*

The *latest* time that a child of A will be born is just before A's death, so the *latest* time that a child of A will reach age X is X years after A's death. Therefore, if we have a contingency that an unborn person must reach age X, all his possible parents will resolve the contingency within X years (not immediately). We insist on saying "all the possible parents" for the same reason we did so for Fact #2; some possible parents may be unborn.

Actually, a child of A will reach age X no later than X years and *9 months* after A's death if A is male and if his wife was pregnant at his death. But this fact does not affect our choice of the parent (A) as the tentative measuring life, because the perpetuities period is extended by an actual period of gestation. The point is illustrated in Example 3-9, § 3.07[C].

If the contingency is that a person who was in being at the time the interest was created must reach age X, we should use Fact #1 instead.

You can see why these facts are useful. They all suggest ways in which the death of a person will resolve a contingency. Therefore, that person should be considered as a measuring life for interests which are subject to that contingency. Note that in each of the examples just given, we stated the *latest* possible time when the contingency will be resolved. That is the time that concerns us because the Rule requires that there be *no possibility* of the interest remaining contingent for too long, and we want to know the *worst* that can happen.

The certainty of vesting or failing that the Rule requires is extremely strict. Under the orthodox application of the Rule, we are required to assume that any person can have children, no matter what his age or sex. It is this "conclusive presumption of fertility" that foreclosed any greater optimism about the latest time for resolving the contingencies in Facts #2 and #3. (See Example 3-8.)

Note that the condition itself may *explicitly state* whose death resolves the contingency. If the remaindermen are "A's issue living at A's death," for example, then the contingency is "A's issue must be living at his death," and obviously A's death will resolve it. (Here, there is also a contingency that unborn issue be born, but that is included in the contingency that they be living at A's death.)

Alternative ways of failing

There is one other thing we must do as part of Step 2. Up to this point our choice for a tentative measuring life was someone whose death would either (1) cause the interest to vest, or (2) cause the interest to fail by precluding the satisfaction of a condition precedent or the birth/ascertainment of an unborn/unascertained person. You will recall, however, that there are *other* ways in which an interest might fail (see § 2.06[B]). Therefore, as a final check for tentative measuring lives, we should see if there is anyone whose death would cause the interest to fail in one of these "alternative" ways. We must be especially vigilant for a life estate, which fails at the death of the life tenant (or other person by whose lifetime the interest is measured). (This point is illustrated in Example 3-15, § 3.07[C].)

If we are unable to find a person or persons whose death(s) resolve *all* the contingencies (or cause the interest to fail in one of the alternative ways), then the interest must be invalid. We should then skip Step 3 and go directly to Step 4 to confirm our conclusion that the interest is bad.

There is an important exception to the preceding paragraph. If an interest is subject to a contingency which must be satisfied, if at all, within 21 years *after the creation of the interest*, then the interest is valid, even though it is not possible to find any person whose death helps to resolve the contingency. See § 3.08[A].

Step 3: Determine whether all the persons found in step 2 were "in being."

"In being" means in existence at the creation of the interest, or in existence at the time a revocable interest became irrevocable. This step is necessary because a person does not qualify as a measuring life unless he was alive when the interest was created.

If we have selected a group of persons as the tentative measuring lives, then all of them must have been in being. For example, if "all of A's children" are the tentative measuring lives, then we must be certain that they were all in existence when the interest was created. (Note, however, that all of A's children would still work as measuring lives if one of A's children had died before the interest was created. When we say that all of A's children must be "in existence" or "in being," we really mean that there must be no possibility that a child of A could be born after the interest was created.)

If we complete steps 1 through 3 successfully, we have found a measuring life, and the interest is valid.

If we are unable to complete steps 1 through 3 successfully, then the interest must be invalid. In that case, we should go on to step 4 to confirm that conclusion.

Step 4: If you are unable to complete Steps 1 through 3, then confirm that no measuring life exists by constructing a counterexample.

This step serves to check our conclusion, reached in Step 2 or 3, that a measuring life cannot be found.

There are two slightly different ways of doing this step, which we label Variations A and B. Only *one* of them need be done; use the one with which you feel most comfortable.

Variation A

First, we make a list of all those persons who were in being and who have even the *slightest* possibility of working as measuring lives. Until you gain more confidence in ruling out persons as measuring lives, your list should include everyone named in the instrument, the parents of all unborn persons described in the instrument, anyone else connected with the instrument, and even anyone else you are not sure about! There is absolutely no harm in being very liberal in making your list; it is impossible to make a mistake by including someone who "should not" have been. As you gain more practice in working with the Rule, you will become better able to see which people could not possibly work as measuring lives and who can, therefore, be omitted from your list.

Then, we produce what we call a "counterexample": a possible sequence of events that would result in the interest remaining contingent more than 21 years after the deaths of *all* the persons on our list. The counterexample will usually be of the following form:

1. An appropriately chosen child is conceived and born.[5]

2. (For some interests) Other events, appropriate to the interest under consideration, occur.

3. Everyone on our list (the people who have even the slightest possibility of working as measuring lives) dies, and the 21-year period begins.

4. Twenty-one years later, when the perpetuities period is over, the interest is still contingent.

In some cases, we will want to precede the birth of the appropriately chosen child in paragraph 1 by the death of an appropriately chosen person.

Producing this sequence of events proves that none of the persons on the list qualifies as a measuring life, because we have established that the interest might not vest or fail within 21 years after all their deaths. Because we listed everyone who could possibly have worked, it must be impossible to find a measuring life.

The child who is born in paragraph 1 and the events in paragraph 2 are chosen for their effect in delaying vesting or failing. As for the newly-born child in paragraph 1, the difficulty we previously encountered in Step 2 or 3 will suggest who he must be. For example, if we selected "all of *A*'s children" as the tentative measuring lives in Step 2, but they did not work as actual measuring lives in Step 3 because they were not necessarily all in being, then the newly-born child that you "produce" in the counterexample should be another child of *A*.

---

[5]This event is unnecessary if the interest is subject to a contingency unconnected with the lifetime of any person and capable of being satisfied in the indefinite future. But the four-step procedure itself is unnecessary for such an interest, which is obviously invalid. (See the Sears Tower example in § 3.05[B].)

You can see why we can (and should) be very liberal in making the list of possible measuring lives at the beginning of Step 4. Including someone on the list who could not possibly work as a measuring life simply results in our formally proving that fact, and no harm is done. This observation suggests a slightly different way of completing Step 4, which we call Variation B.

Variation B

We construct a counterexample in the following form:

1. An appropriately chosen child is conceived and born.[6]

2. (For some interests) Other events, appropriate to the interest under consideration, occur.

3. *Everyone in the world* who was alive when the interest was created dies, and the 21-year period begins.

4. Twenty-one years later, when the perpetuities period is over, the interest is still contingent.

As before, we may want to precede the birth of an appropriately chosen child by the death of an appropriately chosen person, and the child in paragraph 1 and the events in paragraph 2 are chosen for their effect in delaying vesting or failing.

You can see that this is the same method previously outlined, except that here the "list" of potential measuring lives includes everyone in the world alive when the interest was created. They are too numerous to be an actual group of measuring lives (see § 3.06[A] and Example 3-11, § 3.07[C]), but when we imagine the deaths of *everyone* who was "in being," we avoid having to make an actual list of potential measuring lives. Producing the counterexample proves that *no one* alive when the interest was created qualifies as a measuring life.

The disadvantage of Variation B is that you may find it confusing to imagine almost the entire population of the earth dying all at once, and moreover the counterexample may have to include the births of an additional person or two to serve as parents. The disadvantage of Variation A, on the other hand, is that you run the risk of omitting from your list someone who could work as a measuring life. In the remainder of this Guide we will be using Variation B unless we state otherwise.

[C] Applying the four steps

In the following examples, we evaluate the future interests by applying the four steps. In all examples and problems in this book, the facts given are those that existed when the interest was (irrevocably) created. Those are the only facts that we have noted because those are the only facts we are allowed to take into account. You should also assume that all "named" persons (persons identified with letters) were alive when the interest was (irrevocably) created. Any reversion retained by the transferor is valid under the Rule, and we will not make any mention of it.

---

[6]See footnote 5.

Example 3-3
To *A* if he is admitted to the bar.

Facts: *A* has not been admitted to the bar.

Step 1 (state the contingencies): The only contingency is that *A* must be admitted to the bar.

Step 2 (find the tentative measuring lives): Whose death resolves the contingency? Since *A* must do something within his lifetime, *A*'s death will resolve the contingency (Fact #1, § 3.07[B]). *A* is the tentative measuring life.

There is no way in which the interest would fail other than the impossibility of satisfying the condition precedent (there is no "alternative way of failing"; see § 3.07[B]), so there are no other persons to name as tentative measuring lives.

Step 3 (in being?): *A* was in being (we assume that any "named" person was in being).

Therefore, *A*'s interest is valid under the Rule. By the time of his death, either *A* will be a member of the bar (in which case the interest will have vested sometime earlier), or *A* will not have been admitted to the bar and will never be (in which case *A*'s interest will have failed at his death). We do not need the "extra" 21 years after *A*'s death that the Rule allows us. Because we successfully completed Steps 2 and 3, we omit Step 4, which is used only to confirm the *invalidity* of an interest.

Example 3-4
To *X* if *A* is admitted to the bar.

Facts: *A* has not been admitted to the bar.

A works as a measuring life here for exactly the same reason that he works as a measuring life in the previous example. Therefore, *X*'s interest is valid. The fact that *A* is given no interest under the conveyance is irrelevant; we can still use him as a measuring life for *X*'s interest.

X does not work as a measuring life because *X*'s death does not affect the possibility of *A*'s being admitted to the bar. If *X* dies while *A* is still alive but not yet a member of the bar, *X*'s interest will descend to his heirs or will beneficiaries, and it will remain contingent in them.

Example 3-5
To *L* for life, then to *X* if *A* is admitted to the bar.

Facts: *A* has not been admitted to the bar.

The only difference between *X*'s interest in this example and *X*'s interest in the preceding example is that here it is preceded by a life estate. That difference is insignificant for purposes of applying the Rule. Using the analysis already applied in Examples 3-3 and 3-4, *X*'s interest is valid.

Example 3-6
To *A* for life, then to *B* if *B* attains the age of 30.

Facts: *B* is now 2 years old.

Step 1 (state the contingencies): The contingency is that *B* must reach the age of 30.

Step 2 (find the tentative measuring lives): Whose death resolves the contingency? The contingency is of the sort requiring a named, living person to do something during his lifetime, here reaching a designated age. Therefore, *B* is the tentative measuring life (Fact #1, § 3.07[B]). (Note that we do not want to use Fact #3 to help us choose a tentative measuring life, because the person who is required to reach 30 is a specified, living person, not a potentially unborn person.)

There is no alternative way in which the interest would fail, so there are no other persons to name as tentative measuring lives.

Step 3 (in being?): *B* was alive when the interest was created.

Therefore the interest is valid. (Because we successfully completed Steps 2 and 3, we omit Step 4.) You can see that the analysis is substantially the same as that for Example 3-3. The two examples are variations on a theme, because in both of them the contingency is that something must be done during the lifetime of a named, living person.

Example 3-7
To *A* for life, then to *A*'s first child.

Facts: *A* has not had any children.

Step 1 (state the contingencies): The interest in *A*'s first child is contingent because he is not yet born. Therefore, we state the contingency as "A child of *A* must be born."

Step 2 (find the tentative measuring lives): No child of *A* can be born after *A*'s death. At *A*'s death, either *A* will have had a child (the interest will have vested), or *A* will not have had any children and can never have one (the interest will have failed).[7] *A* is the tentative measuring life. (We have used Fact #2, § 3.07[B].)

There is no alternative way in which the interest would fail, so there are no other persons to name as tentative measuring lives.

_____

[7]If *A* is male and his wife is pregnant at his death, *A* can have child after his death. But that is immaterial in this example, and in any event the perpetuities period is extended by actual periods of gestation.

Step 3 (in being?): *A* was alive when the interest was created.

Therefore *A* is the measuring life. The interest in *A*'s first child is valid. (Because we successfully completed Steps 2 and 3, we omit Step 4.)

Example 3-8

To *A* for life, then to the first child of *A* to reach the age of 30.

Facts: *A* has had only two children, *C1* (28 years old) and *C2* (27 years old).

Step 1 (state the contingencies): The contingency is that a child of *A* must reach 30. Note carefully that the remainder is *not* in "the first of *A*'s children *now alive* to reach the age of 30." (Also compare to a conveyance "to the first child of *A*, if he reaches the age of 30." The first child of *A* is *C1*; the remainder would be in him only, not in *C2*.) Because *A* is still alive and can have more children, it is possible that neither *C1* nor *C2* will be the first child of *A* to reach the age of 30. Both of them might die before they reach 30, and the first child of *A* who reaches 30 might be a child born to *A* after the interest was created. To keep this in mind, you might want to state the contingency as "a child of *A*, *whether born or unborn*, must reach the age of 30."

Step 2 (find the tentative measuring lives): The requirement that a child of *A* reach age 30 is a requirement that one of *A*'s children "do something," so we can try to use Fact #1, § 3.07[B], to find a tentative measuring life. The tentative measuring lives are, then, *all* of *A*'s children. (Perhaps you see immediately that "all of *A*'s children" cannot work as *actual* measuring lives because they are not all in being. But we postpone making that observation formally until Step 3.) *C1* and *C2* cannot serve as the tentative measuring lives by themselves, because their deaths do not resolve the contingency of one of *A*'s children reaching age 30. As we have already noted under Step 1, their deaths will not necessarily cut off the possibility that a child of *A* might yet reach 30.

We can also try to use Fact #3. That tells us that *A*'s death will resolve the contingency of a child of his reaching age 30, but *A*'s death will resolve that contingency *within 30 years*. Since *A* can have no more children after his death, the latest that a child of *A* will reach 30 will be 30 years after *A*'s death. But *A*'s death must resolve the contingency *within 21 years* in order for *A* to qualify as a tentative measuring life, so Fact #3 does not help us in finding a tentative measuring life. *A* himself will not work.

There is no alternative way in which the interest could fail, so there are no other persons to name as tentative measuring lives.

Step 3 (in being?): Our tentative measuring lives are all of *A*'s children. But at the time the interest was created, *A* is alive, he can have more children, and therefore all of *A*'s children are *not* necessarily in being. They do not qualify as actual measuring lives.

Step 4 (construct a counterexample): The reason we were unable to complete Step 3 tells us how to construct the counterexample in Step 4. In fact, one might say that we have already done Step 4 implicitly while completing the previous steps, but let us do it now explicitly.

Under Variation A, we list the people who have the slightest possibility of working as measuring lives; they are A, C1, C2, and A's parents (if alive). (After some practice, we will see that A's parents could not possibly work, but there is no harm in including them now.)

The difficulty we identified in Step 3 (all of A's children were not necessarily in being) helps us produce a counterexample now. Let us imagine that the following chain of events takes place.

1. After the instrument takes effect (after the interest was created), A has another child (C3). We take note of the fact that C3 was not in being, so he cannot be a measuring life.[8]

2. Immediately afterwards, all the persons on our list (A, C1, C2, and A's parents) die. Neither C1 nor C2 had reached 30.[9] Because all our proposed measuring lives have died, the 21-year "timer" starts.

3. Twenty-one years later the timer "rings." C3 is still alive, he is 21 years old, and he might reach 30 or he might not. If he reaches 30, he will be "the first child of A to reach the age of 30." *The interest is still contingent at the end of the perpetuities period.*

Although we are by no means certain that the above sequence of events *will* happen, the fact that it *could* happen proves that the persons on our list do not work as measuring lives. Since we chose those persons as the only ones who had even the slightest possibility of working, it must be the case that there is no one who will work. The interest is invalid.

Variation B for Step 4 would proceed in the same way, except that we do not make a list of possible measuring lives, and we imagine that everyone in the world who was alive when the interest was created dies immediately after C3's birth. (For a more complete explanation of the use of Variation B, see Example 3-12, in this section.)

Point of potential confusion
In the conveyance under discussion, it is *not* accurate to say that there are three different contingent remainders, one in

---

[8]C3 was not in being only if he had not yet been conceived when the interest was created. We will assume, each time we refer to the birth of a child after the beginning of the perpetuities period, that the time of conception was also after the beginning of the period.

[9]Since C1 and C2 are close to reaching 30, you may want to "kill them off" as the very first event of your counterexample, even before C3 is born. It is not necessary to do so in this example, but it is often less taxing on our thinking to get persons who might satisfy an age contingency out of the way as soon as possible.

C1, one in *C2*, and one in unborn children of *A*. If that were so, then we could say that *C1*'s interest is good, because he is his own measuring life; and *C2*'s interest is good, because he is his own measuring life; and their interests are not affected by the invalidity of the gift to unborn children of *A* (for which there is no measuring life).[10] But we do *not* have three different remainders. There is only one remainder, and there is only one remainderman, namely, the unascertained person who is "the first child of *A* to reach the age of 30."[11]

The conclusive presumption of fertility

Our conclusion that the interest is invalid is correct even if, at the time the interest was created, *A* was incapable of having more children (for example, because *A* was a female and past the age of childbearing). In exploring what might happen regarding vesting and failing, a long-established interpretation of the Rule requires us to assume that any person of any age can continue to have children.[12] It has become customary to refer to an example which illustrates this principle as the case of the "fertile octogenarian."[13] This "conclusive presumption of fertility" has, not surprisingly, attracted much criticism. However, now that the word "children" in wills and trust instruments is widely construed to include adopted children, the presumption does not seem so absurd.

Example 3-9
To *A* for life, then to the first child of *A* to reach the age of 21.

Facts: *A* has had two children, *C1* (20 years old) and *C2* (18 years old).

Step 1 (state the contingencies): A child of *A* must reach 21.

Step 2 (find the tentative measuring lives): The contingency will be resolved at the deaths of *all* of *A*'s children (Fact #1). We list "all of *A*'s children" as tentative measuring lives. We cannot say that the contingency will be resolved at the deaths of *C1* and *C2*, for the same reason we could not do so in the previous example.

---

[10]This is not a class gift and therefore is not subject to the "all-or-nothing rule" (§ 4.02).

[11]But compare the subclass exception to the all-or-nothing rule (§ 4.04[A]) and the doctrine of "splitting the contingencies" (§ 6.03).

[12]The leading case is *Jee v. Audley*, 1 Cox 324, 29 Eng. Rep. 1186 (Ch. 1787).

[13]The term was probably first used by Professor Leach. Leach, *Perpetuities in a Nutshell*, 51 Harv. L. Rev. 638, 643 (1938).

Also, the contingency will be resolved 21 years after *A*'s death (Fact #3). Unlike the previous example, here *A*'s death resolves the contingency "soon enough" to qualify him as a tentative measuring life.

Step 3 (in being?): Because *A* was alive when the interest was created, *A* could have more children. "All of *A*'s children" were not necessarily in being, and they do not work as actual measuring lives.

However, we also listed *A* himself as a tentative measuring life. He *was* in being, so he qualifies as an actual measuring life. We only need *one* measuring life, so the fact that "all of *A*'s children" did not qualify is immaterial in this example.

We have successfully completed all three steps and found a measuring life, so the interest is valid.

Extension of the perpetuities period by a period of gestation

Note that the latest time that a child of *A* can reach 21 is actually 21 years *and 9 months* after *A*'s death. That would occur if *A* was male and he conceived a child just before his death. But *A* can still work as a measuring life, even though the contingency might not be resolved until 21 years *and 9 months* after *A*'s death, because the perpetuities period is extended by an actual period of gestation.

We could redraw our previous diagram of the perpetuities period (§ 3.04) to show how the perpetuities period is extended in this example. (Again, the diagram is not to scale.)

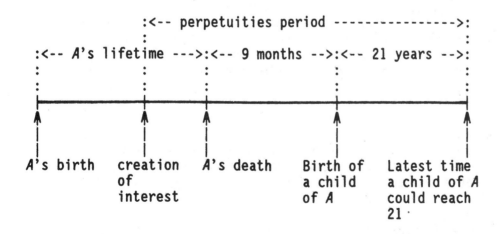

Example 3-10
T makes a devise to *T*'s grandchildren who are living 21 years after the deaths of *A*, *B*, *C*, *D*, *E*, and *F*.

Step 1 (state the contingencies): The contingency is that *T*'s grandchildren must be living 21 years after the deaths of the named persons. (For unborn grandchildren, the contingency that they must be living at a certain time includes the contingency that they must be born before then.)

Step 2 (find the tentative measuring lives): Here, the devise tells us *explicitly* whose deaths resolve the contingency. Obviously, the deaths of *A*, *B*, *C*, *D*, *E*, and *F* will resolve the contingency within 21 years.

A contingency that a grandchild must be alive at a certain time is resolved by the grandchild's death. By the time a grandchild dies, either he will have satisfied the requirement, or he will never satisfy it. (This is another application of Fact #1, § 3.07[B].) Therefore, we ought to list all the grandchildren as tentative measuring lives as well.

Step 3 (in being?): The perpetuities period starts at *T*'s death, when his devise takes effect. Assuming that *A*, *B*, *C*, *D*, *E*, and *F* were all in being at that time (and we shall assume throughout this book that "named" persons were in being), they work as measuring lives. The interest is valid.

If *T* died survived by one or more children, then more of *T*'s grandchildren can be born after his death. Therefore, all of *T*'s grandchildren were not necessarily in being. Because we already have *A*, *B*, *C*, *D*, *E*, and *F* as measuring lives, the fact that the grandchildren do not work is irrelevant. (If, on the other hand, *T* was not survived by children, then all his grandchildren were in being at his death, and they would work as measuring lives.)

This example raises an issue about the permissible number of measuring lives. In the typical conveyance, the contingencies are resolved by the deaths of relatives of the transferor. However, some transferors, in an attempt to postpone distribution of trust property for as long as possible, specify that the trust is to terminate (and the contingencies be resolved) at the deaths of a number of persons named in the instrument, as in the example we just considered. How many persons may be named? Could the transferor in the above example have listed twenty persons instead of the six? Is the following conveyance valid?

> **Example 3-11**
> *T* makes a bequest in trust, income to *L* for life, then principal to *T*'s issue who are living 21 years after the deaths of all the people listed in the Manhattan telephone book who are alive at *T*'s death.

The interest in the issue is invalid. The precise reason for the invalidity of the interest is not clear from the cases, however. One theory seems to be that the Rule does not permit the number of measuring lives to be so large that it would be unreasonably difficult to discover when the last one of them dies. Since the Rule itself does not require that we know how long the measuring lives actually live, this theory is not very convincing. Another theory is that a future interest like this is void *for uncertainty*: it would be unreasonably difficult, not to say impossible, to know when all the persons listed in the Manhattan telephone book have died, and therefore we will not be able to know when, or to whom, to distribute the principal. It does not matter which theory we use; under either theory the interest is invalid. (We cannot use T's issue themselves as the measuring lives because they were not all in being.)

If the testator had listed twenty persons, the interest would probably have been valid. An oft-cited case involving the issue at hand is *In Re Villar*,[14] in which the court held valid a devise which was to remain contingent until 20 years after the deaths of all of Queen Victoria's descendants who were alive at the testator's death. There were at least 120 such descendants alive four years before the testator's death. The court, stating that the issue was whether the disposition was "void for uncertainty, or, in other words, that it was impracticable," held the interest valid. It has been suggested that the court was influenced by the relative ease of discovering the whereabouts of a queen's descendants. Moreover, the devise was taken from a form book, and a holding of invalidity would have cast doubt on many other similar devises.[15]

Example 3-12
To A for life, then to A's first grandchild.

Facts: A has had one child, $C1$, but no grandchildren.

Step 1 (state the contingencies): The contingency is that a grandchild of A must be born.

Step 2 (find the tentative measuring lives): That contingency will be resolved at the deaths of the parents of that potential grandchild, namely, *all* of A's children (Fact #2, § 3.07[B]). It is important to note that the remainder is *not* in the first child of $C1$ (who would be a grandchild of A). The conveyance does not specify that the grandchild must be $C1$'s child; it could be a child of *another* child of A (born after the conveyance).

There is no alternative way in which the interest could fail, so there are no other persons to name as tentative measuring lives. (We will not continue to note this.)

Step 3 (in being?): Since A is still alive, he can have more children. Therefore, the tentative measuring lives, "all of A's children," are not necessarily in being. The interest is invalid. We continue with Step 4 to check our conclusion.

Step 4 (construct a counterexample): Again, the reason that we failed to successfully complete Step 3 tells us how to construct the counterexample. This time we shall use Variation B of Step 4. The following sequence of events might happen.

1. A has another child, $C2$. (We know that this is one of the events in the counterexample because the possibility that A might have another child was precisely the problem we encountered in Step 3.) We note that $C2$, born

---

[14]1 Ch. 243 (1929).

[15]L. Simes and A. Smith, The Law of Future Interests § 1223, at 111 (2d ed. 1956).

(and, we assume, conceived) after the interest was created, is not a life in being.

2. Everyone in the world alive when the interest was created dies, and the 21-year "timer" starts.

3. Twenty-one years later, when the timer rings, C2 is still alive, and he still might have a child (who would be A's first grandchild). We are at the end of the perpetuities period, and there is still a contingent interest in "A's first grandchild."

The counterexample shows that *none* of the persons alive when the interest was created can qualify as measuring lives, because we have just imagined one possible sequence of events in which the interest would remain contingent 21 years after the deaths of all of those persons. Therefore, it is impossible to find a measuring life, and the interest is invalid.

Of course, C2 can have a child (A's first grandchild) only if there is someone else alive who can serve as the other parent. Therefore, a more complete statement of the counterexample would be as follows (the language we have added is italicized):

1. *A* has another child, *C2*. *S, an unrelated person, is born.*

2. Everyone in the world alive when the interest was created dies, and the 21-year "timer" starts.

3. Twenty-one years later, when the timer rings, C2 is still alive, *he might marry S*, and he still might have a child (who would be A's first grandchild). We are at the end of the perpetuities period, and there is still a contingent interest in "A's first grandchild."

But it is easier simply to recognize that our counterexamples do not purport to state *everything* that happens after the interest was created. We should assume (and we will assume in the rest of this book) that *every* counterexample implicitly includes the birth of some unrelated persons after the interest was created. These persons do not die when "Everyone in the world *alive when the interest was created* dies." In this way our counterexamples will always include a "supply" of parents whom we can use if necessary. On the other hand, if you find all this too confusing, then you can use Variation A of Step 4 instead.

Example 3-13
O makes a bequest to A for life, then to O's first grandchild.

Facts: O has not had any grandchildren, and he is survived by children.

Step 1 (state the contingency): A grandchild of O must be born.

Step 2 (find the tentative measuring lives): The persons whose deaths will resolve the contingency that a grandchild of O must be born are all the possible parents of that grandchild (Fact #2, § 3.07[B]), *i.e.*, all of O's children.

Step 3 (in being?): Note that the example involves a *bequest*, a transfer under *O*'s will. The interest in *O*'s first grandchild is not created until *O*'s will takes effect, at his death. The facts we can take into account are those existing when the interest was created, at *O*'s death. At that time, *O* cannot have any more children. Therefore, we can say that the tentative measuring lives, "all of *O*'s children," *are* in being. It is true that a child of *O* may have predeceased him, and in that case one of *O*'s children would not be "in being" at *O*'s death. But here, and elsewhere in this book, when we say that someone's children are all "in being," we mean that no other children can be born. There is always the possibility that a child may have already died, but that is not significant for purposes of the Rule. Here, therefore, *O*'s children work as the actual measuring lives. The interest is valid.

Of course, if we know who *O*'s children are, we can describe the measuring lives by listing the names of the children instead of saying "all of *O*'s children." If *O* was survived neither by children nor grandchildren, the interest in grandchildren would fail, but not because of invalidity under the Rule against Perpetuities.

Note that all of *O*'s children work as measuring lives even though they are given no interest and, indeed, are not even mentioned in the instrument.

There *is* a possibility that not all of *O*'s children were in being at his death. If *O* is male and his wife is pregnant at his death, one of *O*'s children will be born after his death. But this possibility does not prevent us from saying that "all of *O*'s children" were in being and can serve as the measuring lives. A person who has been conceived but not yet born is considered "in being" and can serve as a measuring life. In this example, even if one of *O*'s children is born after his death, that child can serve as one of the measuring lives along with his brothers and sisters.

We saw in Example 3-9, in this section, that the perpetuities period is lengthened by a period of gestation. If you find it helpful to do so, you can imagine that the perpetuities period has been extended by a period of gestation in Example 3-13 as well. Suppose that *O*'s first child, *C1*, was conceived just before *O*'s death. In this case, the measuring lives, "all of *O*'s children," would simply be *C1*, and we could diagram the perpetuities period as follows. (Again, the diagram is not to scale.)

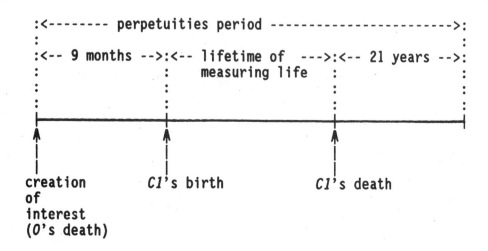

```
:<-------- perpetuities period ----------------------->:
:                                                       :
:<-- 9 months -->:<-- lifetime of  --->:<-- 21 years -->:
:                :      measuring life :                :
:                :                     :                :
:                :                     :                :
:                :                     :                :
|----------------|---------------------|----------------|
↑                ↑                     ↑
|                |                     |
|                |                     |
creation         C1's birth            C1's death
of
interest
(O's death)
```

Here, we can imagine that the period of gestation has extended the perpetuities period at its beginning (rather than at its end, as in Example 3-9). That is simply another way of stating that a person conceived but not yet born can serve as a measuring life.

Example 3-14
To *A* for life, then to *B*'s first child if that child marries.

Facts: *B* has not had any children.

Step 1 (state the contingencies):
Contingency #1. *B*'s first child must be born.
Contingency #2. That child must marry.

Step 2 (find the tentative measuring lives): As for the first contingency, *B* is the tentative measuring life (Fact #2, § 3.07[B]). As for the second contingency, *B*'s first child is the tentative measuring life (Fact #1). (Note that the only child who can take is *B*'s first child. Therefore, it is most appropriate to describe the tentative measuring life as "*B*'s first child." If, on the other hand, the interest had been in "the first child of *B* to marry," then any of *B*'s children, not just the first-born, might be entitled to take. In that case, we would describe the tentative measuring lives as "all of *B*'s children.")

Note that *B* himself cannot serve as the tentative measuring life for the second contingency, because *B*'s death does not prevent (or cause) the marriage of his children. Put another way, a child of *B* can be married more than 21 years after *B*'s death.

Step 3 (in being?): As for the first contingency, *B* was in being and can serve as the measuring life. As for the second contingency, *B*'s first child was not in being. We have not been able to find measuring lives for *both* contingencies, and the interest is invalid. We go to Step 4 to confirm our conclusion.

Step 4 (construct a counterexample): The following events could occur:

1. *B* has a child, *C1*. (Note that he was not in being.)

2. Everyone in the world who was alive when the interest was created dies, and the 21-year timer starts to count down.

3. Twenty-one years later, *C1* is still alive and unmarried, but he still might marry. The interest is still contingent at the end of the perpetuities period.

Example 3-15
To *A* for life, then to *B* for life if one of *B*'s children is admitted to the bar, then to *C*.

Facts: *B* has children, but none of them has been admitted to the bar.

C is born and ascertained, and there is no condition precedent for *C*'s interest. Therefore, *C*'s interest is vested, and it is valid under the Rule. We next evaluate *B*'s interest.

Step 1 (state the contingencies): *B*'s interest is subject to the condition precedent that one of his children must be admitted to the bar.

Step 2 (find the tentative measuring lives): The contingency will be resolved by the deaths of all of *B*'s children (Fact #1).

Here, however, there *is* a way in which the interest would fail other than the impossibility of satisfying the condition precedent. *B* has a life estate, and therefore his interest will fail at his death. (If, prior to *B*'s death, the condition precedent had been satisfied and *B* was in possession, we would probably not use the word "fail" to describe the ending of *B*'s interest, but that is of no consequence for perpetuities analysis.) We must list *B* as a tentative measuring life.

Step 3 (in being?): Because *B* was alive when the interest was created, "all of *B*'s children" were not necessarily in being, and they cannot serve as measuring lives.

However, *B* was in being, and he can serve as a measuring life. At *B*'s death, we will not necessarily have resolved the contingency that one of his children must be admitted to the bar. But it is immaterial that the contingency might still be unresolved at that time, because *B*'s interest will lose its contingent character by simply disappearing. The interest is valid.

A life estate in a person who was in being will *always* be valid, regardless of the contingencies to which it may be subject. We will always be able to use the life beneficiary himself as the measuring life. (If it is a life estate pur autre vie, the person by whose lifetime the estate is measured will be the measuring life.)

§ 3.08 Some special cases

[A] Interests certain to vest or fail within the 21-year "period in gross"

In the examples that we have discussed so far, we have seen that the interest will be invalid if we cannot find a person whose death causes the interest to vest or fail immediately or within another 21 years. There is an important exception to this principle.

The exception can best be understood by a short review. By now we are very familiar with the fact that an interest must surely vest or fail within a period of time that is made up of two components: (1) the lifetime of a person in existence when the interest was created, and (2) another 21 years. The reason we try to find a "measuring life," of course, is that his lifetime represents the *first* component of the perpetuities period.

But suppose we can prove that a particular interest will surely vest or fail within 21 years *after the creation of the interest*. In that case, the first component of the perpetuities period--the lifetime of the measuring life--is unnecessary. The second component of 21 years, alone, is all the time that the interest "requires" for vesting or failing. Because we have no need of the first component of the perpetuities period, we do not need to find a measuring life to prove the validity of the interest.

In summary, then, the principle is this. Even if we *cannot* find a measuring life using the four-step procedure, the interest will *still* be valid if we can prove that it will vest or fail within 21 years after the creation of the interest. And *that* will be possible only if *the instrument explicitly states that the contingency must be resolved within the next 21 years.*

> **Example 3-16**
> To *A*, but if liquor is served on the property at any time during the next 21 years, to *B*.
>
> Facts: Liquor has not been served on the property.

A's interest, being a present interest, is valid. We look at *B*'s interest. The condition "but if liquor is served on the property at any time during the next 21 years" is a condition precedent *as to B's interest* (see § 2.04[A]). Under Step 1, we would say that liquor must be served during that period.[16] There is no person whose death *causes* liquor to be served on the property (immediately or within 21 years), nor is there anyone whose death *prevents* liquor from being served on the property. Therefore, we would not be able to find a tentative measuring life for *B*'s interest under Step 2. However, the contingency will be resolved no later than 21 years after the date the instrument took effect. If liquor has not been served by the time that 21-year period has elapsed, the condition will never be satisfied, and *B*'s interest will fail. Therefore, to resolve the contingency, we do not need a measuring life; the 21-year portion of the perpetuities period is enough. *B*'s interest is valid. Another way of explaining this result is to say that *any* person in existence when the interest was created will work as a measuring life.

The example illustrates something about the perpetuities period which has been implicit in all our work so far. Note that the 21-year period of time within which we are certain *B*'s interest will vest or fail does *not* represent the period of minority of a particular child (nor, for that matter, does it have any other connection with any person). The 21-year component of the perpetuities period is sometimes called a "period in gross" to describe the fact that no such connection is required.

---

[16]Remember that when *B* dies, his interest passes to his heirs or will beneficiaries; there is no condition of survivorship.

If the instrument specifies that the contingency might not be resolved for a period *longer* than 21 years, then the analysis just given would not work, and the interest would be invalid.

It will be obvious when you can apply the principle discussed in this section, because the instrument will explicitly refer to a period of time which is 21 years or less.

[B] Executory interests certain to become present estates

Example 3-17
O conveys land "to *A* 30 years from now."

A's interest is certain to become a present estate 30 years from the date of the conveyance. Either *A* himself will be entitled to possession at that time, or if *A* dies in the meantime, then *A*'s heirs or will beneficiaries will be entitled to possession. The "condition" (the passage of 30 years) is one that is *certain* to occur, so it does not appear to be a condition precedent. Also, *A* is born and ascertained. *A*'s interest does not appear to be contingent.

Nevertheless, traditionally we do not call *A*'s interest vested. *A* has an executory interest (of the "springing" type). Unlike remainders, executory interests are said to be "vested" *only* when they become present possessory interests. In the example, *A*'s interest will not become "vested" in this sense until 30 years have elapsed. But we have already decided that *A*'s interest ought not to be called contingent either. *A*'s interest is simply "non-vested."

How does the Rule apply to *A*'s interest? There are no persons whose deaths will resolve the "condition" of 30 years passing by, and clearly *A*'s interest will not become vested, under the traditional view, until after the 21-year period in gross has expired. Accordingly, Professor Gray said that *A*'s interest is invalid under the Rule.[17]

On the other hand, others have taken a more realistic view of the situation. The Rule is concerned with interests remaining contingent for too long, and *A*'s interest is no more contingent than a vested remainder after a life estate (and it probably ties up the underlying property to a lesser degree). The more recent view seems to be that the interest is good under the Rule.[18]

The analogous interest in personal property is treated as vested ("vested with postponed enjoyment"; see § 2.04[C][1]).[19]

---

[17]J. Gray, The Rule Against Perpetuities § 201, at 191 n. 3 (4th ed. 1942).

[18]See, for example, 6 American Law of Property § 24.20 (A. Casner ed. 1952).

[19]T. Bergin and P. Haskell, Preface to Estates in Land and Future Interests 205 n. 80 (2d ed. 1984).

[C] Invalidity of executory interests

We said earlier that the effect of finding an interest invalid under the Rule is that the interest never existed. We can visualize this result by pretending that we take a pen and draw a line through the words which purported to create the invalid interest. This can be tricky, however, in two kinds of cases involving executory interests.

[1] Fee simple determinable compared with fee simple subject to an executory limitation

Earlier we made the distinction between a special limitation and a condition subsequent. That distinction causes a difference in result under the Rule.

> **Example 3-18**
> O conveys "to the First Universalist Society, so long as the land shall be used for purposes of the Society; and when it shall be diverted from those uses, then to A."[20]

There is no person whose death has any effect on whether the land is used for purposes of the Society, nor will that contingency be resolved within 21 years. Therefore, A's interest is void under the Rule. We must strike all the words which describe A's interest in order to determine what interests have actually been created. Clearly, the words "then to A" describe A's interest and are stricken. Equally clearly, the words "to the First Universalist Society" describe the Society's interest, not A's interest, and they are retained.

The difficulty lies in deciding whether to strike the language of condition. O's intent that the land be used for purposes of the Society is expressed *twice*, once in the clause which starts with "so long as" and once in the clause which starts with "and when." The first clause, which describes when the Society's right of possession ends, states a "special limitation" and has the effect of creating a fee simple determinable in the First Universalist Society (see § 2.02[B]). *A special limitation is thought to be an inherent part of the fee simple determinable*; in a sense, the "so long as" phrase "belongs" to the Society's interest, not to A's interest. That means we do *not* strike the phrase when we find that A's interest is invalid.

We would probably say that the second clause, the one beginning "and when," describes when A's right of possession begins and "belongs" to A's interest. When we strike the language creating A's interest, we should probably strike that clause as well. (It doesn't really much matter; the important thing is that the Society's interest is still subject to the "so long as" language.)

The result is as if the grantor had written, "to the First Universalist Society, so long as the land shall be used for purposes of the Society." The grantor has retained a possibility of reverter, which is not subject to the Rule, and he will be entitled to possession if the Society's interest ends. In other words, unless we can find some other

---

[20]If A's interest were valid, it would be an executory interest.

indication of the grantor's intent, we infer from the grantor's language that he wanted the Society's interest to terminate when the land is no longer used for purposes of the Society, *regardless of whether the interest in A can take effect.*

The example is based on *First Universalist Society v. Boland.*[21]

> **Example 3-19**
> *O* conveys "to the Church in Brattle Square, upon the condition that the property is used as the residence of the minister; and in case the property is not so used, then to my nephew."[22]

The nephew's interest is invalid under the Rule, for the same sort of reasons that *A*'s interest in the previous example was invalid. Therefore, we can imagine striking the words which describe his interest. The words "to the Church in Brattle Square" obviously describe the Church's interest and remain; the words "then to my nephew" describe the nephew's interest and are stricken. Again, the difficult decision is whether to strike the words of condition.

The condition is introduced by the words "upon the condition that." This is the sort of language that creates a "condition subsequent" rather than a special limitation (§ 2.02[C]). Therefore, the interest in the Church is not a fee simple determinable but rather a fee simple subject to a condition subsequent. (More precisely, the condition is an executory limitation, and the Church's interest is a fee simple subject to an executory limitation. See § 2.02[D].) In discussing the previous example, we said that a special limitation is thought to be an inherent part of the fee simple determinable. But a condition subsequent is viewed differently. We think of it as something extrinsic to the preceding interest (in the Church) and belonging more to the succeeding interest (in the nephew). Therefore, when we strike the words that purported to create the nephew's (invalid) interest, we strike all the words of condition as well. We are left only with the words "to the Church in Brattle Square." The surprising result is that *the Church has a fee simple absolute.* Although the Rule does not apply to the Church's interest because it is a present interest, the Rule does have the effect of "changing" it when the nephew's interest is invalidated. (Of course, the Church's interest was not *really* changed, because the nephew's interest was never there. The Church's interest was a fee simple absolute all along.)

Another way of saying the same thing is that the Church's fee simple subject to a condition subsequent (or fee simple subject to an executory limitation) does not end by its own terms; it ends only because the following interest cuts it short. If the following interest is not really there, because it is invalid, then the Church's interest is not cut short after all.

---

[21] 155 Mass. 171, 29 N.E. 524 (1892). See also *City of Klamath Falls v. Bell,* 7 Or.App. 330, 490 P.2d 515 (1971), and *Brown v. Independent Baptist Church of Woburn,* 325 Mass. 645, 91 N.E.2d 922 (1950).

[22] If the nephew's interest were valid, it would be an executory interest.

This result supposedly reflects the transferor's intent (again, unless there are indications to the contrary) that he wanted the condition to terminate the Church's interest only if the nephew could take.

The example is taken from *Proprietors of the Church in Brattle Square v. Grant*,[23] the leading case on this point.

[2] Contingent remainder compared with vested remainder subject to complete divestment

In our review of estates and future interests, not only did we point out the subtle distinction between a condition subsequent and a special limitation, but we also noted the difference between a condition subsequent and a condition precedent. That difference, too, may affect the operation of the Rule. Compare the following two examples.

Example 3-20
To *A* for life, then to *B*'s first child if that child marries.

Facts: *B* has not had any children.

We saw earlier that the interest in *B*'s first child is invalid (see Example 3-14, § 3.07[C]).

Example 3-21
To *A* for life, then to *B*'s first child, but if that child does not marry, to *C*.

Facts: *B* has not had any children.

The condition "but if that child does not marry" is a *condition subsequent with respect to the interest in B's first child*, not a condition precedent (Example 2-12, § 2.04[A]). (More precisely, it is an executory limitation.) The only contingency for that child's interest, therefore, is that he must be born. *B*'s death will resolve the contingency that his first child must be born, and therefore *B* is the tentative measuring life. Since *B* was in being, *B* is the actual measuring life, and the interest in *B*'s first child is good.

The condition "but if that child does not marry" is a *condition precedent with respect to C's interest*: *C* is not entitled to possession unless the condition is met. The contingency for *C*'s interest is, of course, that *B*'s first child must not marry. This is just the *reverse* of the contingency for the interest in the previous example, and *C*'s interest is invalid for the same kind of reason that the interest in *B*'s first child was invalid in that previous example.

---

[23]69 Mass. (3 Gray) 142 (1855).

To see the effect of the invalidity of *C*'s interest, we pretend that we cross off the language that purported to create it. It is obvious that the words "to *C*" describe *C*'s interest, and they should be crossed off.

In deciding whether to cross off the words "but if that child does not marry," we use an analysis similar to that given in the preceding subsection. We noted in Example 3-19 that the words "upon the condition that the property is used as the residence of the minister" belonged to the *following* interest, and not to the interest in the Church. In the same way, the words "but if that child does not marry" "belong" to *C*'s interest, not to the interest in *B*'s first child. As a result, we must strike them when we strike *C*'s interest, and *B*'s first child's interest is no longer subject to any condition. (We might also explain this result by saying that *B*'s interest cannot be divested if the divesting interest is invalid.) The Rule has not just invalidated *C*'s interest; it has also "changed" *B*'s first child's interest from a remainder that is vested (once he is born) subject to complete divestment to a remainder that is absolutely vested (again, once he is born).

§ 3.09 More on the meaning of "certainty" under the Rule

We have said that the Rule is satisfied only if we can be *certain* that the interest will vest or fail by the end of the period. Conversely, the Rule is violated if there is *any possibility, no matter how unlikely*, that the interest might still be contingent at that time. We have already seen one example of the "certainty" required by the Rule: the presumed fact that any person, regardless of his age or sex, is capable of having more children (Example 3-8, § 3.07[C]).

The following examples further illustrate the "certainty" which the Rule requires.

[A] The "unborn widow"

> **Example 3-22**
> *O* conveys in trust, income to *O*'s son for life, then income to the son's widow for life, then principal to the son's first child if he is then living.

Facts: *O*'s son is married but has had no children.

Let us evaluate the interest in the son's first child.

Step 1 (state the contingencies):
Contingency #1. The son's first child must be born.
Contingency #2. The son's first child must be alive at the death of the son's widow or, if the son dies unmarried, at the son's death.[24]

---

[24]We might choose to state only contingency #2, since he cannot be alive at a particular time unless he has been born before then.

Step 2 (find the tentative measuring lives): The first contingency will be resolved at the son's death.

The second contingency will be resolved at the death of the son's widow or the death of the son. Surviving to a particular time is something that the son's first child can accomplish only during his lifetime, so we ought to list him as a tentative measuring life as well.

Step 3 (in being?): As for the first contingency, the son was in being, so he can serve as the measuring life for that contingency.

As for the second contingency, the son's first child was not in being. The son was in being, but the son's first child might be required to survive until the widow's death, so the widow must qualify as a measuring life also. However, the widow was *not* necessarily in being. A widow is the person to whom a man is married at the time of his death. The son's widow will not necessarily be the son's present wife; their marriage might be terminated by divorce or the wife's death, and the son might be married to a different woman at the time of his death. Because the son's widow could be anyone, we cannot be certain that she is even someone who was alive at the creation of the interest. Therefore, the "son's widow" was not in being and cannot serve as a measuring life; the interest is void.

Step 4 (construct a counterexample): Since the problem is that the widow was not necessarily in being, the counterexample produces such a widow, as follows:

1. The son divorces his present wife.

2. A girl, W2, is conceived and born (note that she is not a life in being).

3. The son marries W2, and they have a child, *C1* (he is the son's first child).

4. Everyone in the world who was alive when the interest was created dies. Now the 21-year timer starts to count down.

5. Twenty-one years later, W2 is still alive, *C1* is still alive, and we still do not know whether he will be alive at her death. *C1*'s interest is still contingent at the end of the period.

The interest is invalid even if, given the son's age in a particular case, the likelihood of the son marrying a woman not yet born is very small. The example is called the case of the "unborn widow."

[B] Administrative contingencies: "Upon settlement of my estate"

> ### Example 3-23
> *T* makes a bequest "to the four chair officers of San Diego Lodge No. 168 Benevolent and Protective Order of Elks who are in office at the time of distribution of my estate."[25]

The "time of distribution of my estate" refers to the time when the executor or administrator of *T*'s estate, after his death, distributes *T*'s property to the beneficiaries under his will. The contingency is that the legatees be in office when the testator's estate is distributed. But there is no person whose death will cause, or preclude, the distribution of *T*'s estate, and the four chair officers at the time of distribution need not be persons who were in being at *T*'s death. Therefore there is no tentative measuring life. The interest will be valid only if it will certainly vest or fail within the 21-year "period in gross" portion of the perpetuities period (§ 3.08[A]). While the estate of a testator is typically wound up and distributed much earlier than 21 years after his death, there is no assurance that this will happen. Therefore, the interest is invalid; the extreme unlikelihood that *T*'s estate will not be distributed for 21 years after his death is irrelevant.

[C] The magic gravel pits

> ### Example 3-24
> *T* devised some gravel pits in trust, the trustees to mine the gravel until the pits are exhausted, then to sell the pits and divide the proceeds among the testator's issue then living.

The contingency for the issue's interest is that they must be living when the pits are exhausted.[26] Obviously, that contingency will be resolved only when the pits are exhausted (the issue cannot serve as their own measuring lives because they are not necessarily all in being). There is no person in being whose death has any effect on how fast the gravel will be mined. Therefore, the interest will be good if, and only if, the pits are certain to become exhausted within 21 years after the interest takes effect, *i.e.*, 21 years after the testator's death (§ 3.08[A]). Since it is impossible to know, at the testator's death, how long it will take to remove all the gravel, the interest must be invalid. That was the holding in an actual case with these facts.[27] Evidence showed

---

[25]Based upon *In re Campbell's Estate*, 28 Cal. App. 2d 102, 82 P.2d 22 (1938).

[26]One might say that there is also a contingency that unborn issue must be born, but the requirement that they be living at a particular time includes the requirement that they be born.

We assume that the subclass exception (§ 4.04[A]) would not apply to save the gift as to some of the testator's issue; that would be a very unlikely holding.

[27]*In re Wood*, 3 Ch. 381 (1894).

that, if the rate at which the pits had been mined during the testator's lifetime had continued after his death, the pits would have been exhausted in 3 or 4 years, and they were actually exhausted within 6 years. But, as we know, what is likely to happen or what actually happened is irrelevant.

§ 3.10 Problems for Chapter 3

Are the following interests valid? Unless stated otherwise, assume that all persons identified by capital letters are in being and that any conditions precedent have not been met. Answers begin on page

Problem 3-1
To *A* if he marries.

Problem 3-2
To *A* if he has a child.

Problem 3-3
To *A* if *B* is elected to public office.

Problem 3-4
To *A* if *B* has a daughter.

Problem 3-5
To *A* if *B* finds a cure for cancer.

Problem 3-6
To *A* if anyone finds a cure for cancer.

Problem 3-7
To *A* if anyone finds a cure for cancer during *B*'s lifetime.

Problem 3-8
To *A* if any of *B*'s children finds a cure for cancer.

Facts: *B* is dead.

Problem 3-9
To *A* if any of *A*'s children finds a cure for cancer.

Problem 3-10
O conveys in trust to pay the principal to *O*'s first child, if that child marries.

Facts: The trust is revocable by *O* until his death. At the time of the conveyance, *O* had not had any children. At the time of *O*'s death, *O* had one child, *C1*.

Problem 3-11
O conveys in trust to pay the principal to *O*'s first child, if that child marries.

Facts: The trust is irrevocable. At the time of the conveyance, *O* had not had any children. At the time of *O*'s death, *O* had one child, *C1*.

Problem 3-12
O makes a bequest in trust to pay the principal to *O*'s first child, if that child marries.

Facts: When *O*'s will was executed, *O* had not had any children. At the time of *O*'s death, *O* had one child, *C1*.

Problem 3-13
To *A* for life, then to *A*'s first child if he reaches 21.

Facts: *A* has not had any children.

Problem 3-14
T makes a bequest to the first grandchild of his to reach the age of 25 after *T*'s death.

Facts: *T* was survived by two children, *C1* and *C2*, and one grandchild, *G1*, aged 24.[28]

Problem 3-15
To *A* for life, then to *A*'s first child for life, then to *B*'s first child.[29]

Facts: *A* has had no children; *B* has had no children.

Problem 3-16
To the first grandchild of *A* who reaches 21.

Facts: All of *A*'s children have died. None of *A*'s grandchildren has reached 21, but one grandchild, *G1*, is 20 years old.

---

[28]From L. Simes and A. Smith, The Law of Future Interests § 1228, at 118 (2d ed. 1956).

[29]*Id.*, § 1233, at 137 (2d ed. 1956).

Problem 3-17
To the first grandchild of *A* who reaches 21.

Facts: No grandchild of *A* has reached 21. *A* is dead. *A*'s child, *C1*, is alive. *A*'s grandchild, *G1*, is alive. *G1* is the son of *A*'s child, *C2*, who died before the conveyance was made.

Problem 3-18
O makes a bequest to his first grandchild if he reaches 21.

Facts: At the time of *O*'s death, he had not had any grandchildren.

Problem 3-19
To *A* for life, then to *A*'s first grandchild for life, then to *B*.

Facts: *A* has not had any grandchildren.

§ 3.11 Answers to Problems for Chapter 3

Problems begin on page

Answer to Problem 3-1
Step 1. *A* must be married.

Step 2. He can be married only during his lifetime; *A*'s death will resolve that contingency; *A* is the tentative measuring life.

Step 3. *A* was in being. The interest is valid.

Answer to Problem 3-2
Step 1. A child of *A* must be born.

Step 2. The parent of the unborn child is *A*; *A* is the tentative measuring life.

Step 3. *A* was in being. The interest is valid.

Answer to Problem 3-3
Step 1. *B* must be elected to public office.

Step 2. *B* can be elected to public office only during his lifetime; *B* is the tentative measuring life.

Step 3. *B* was in being. The interest is valid.

Answer to Problem 3-4
Step 1. A daughter must be born to *B*.

Step 2. *B* is the parent of the unborn daughter; *B* is the tentative measuring life.

Step 3. *B* was in being. The interest is valid.

Answer to Problem 3-5
Step 1. *B* must find a cure for cancer.

Step 2. *B* can find a cure for cancer only during his lifetime. *B* is the tentative measuring life.

Step 3. *B* was in being. The interest is valid.

Answer to Problem 3-6
Step 1. Someone must find a cure for cancer.

Step 2. There is no one whose death resolves that contingency. There are no tentative measuring lives. The interest is invalid.

Answer to Problem 3-7
Step 1. Someone must find a cure for cancer during *B*'s lifetime.

Step 2. That can occur only during *B*'s lifetime; *B* is the tentative measuring life.

Step 3. *B* was in being. The interest is valid.

Answer to Problem 3-8
Step 1. One of *B*'s children must find a cure for cancer.

Step 2. A child of *B* can find a cure for cancer only during his lifetime; all of *B*'s children are the tentative measuring lives.

Step 3. Since *B* is dead, all of *B*'s children were in being. The interest is good.

Answer to Problem 3-9
Step 1. One of *A*'s children must find a cure for cancer.

Step 2. They can do so only during their lifetimes; all of *A*'s children (whether born or unborn) are the tentative measuring lives.

Step 3. *A* is alive; not all of *A*'s children are necessarily in being. The interest is invalid.

Step 4. The following events could occur:
1. *A* has another child, *C1*.
2. Everyone in the world who was alive when the interest was created dies. (When *A* dies, his interest passes to his heirs or will beneficiaries.)
3. Twenty-one years later, *C1* is still alive, he could still find a cure for cancer, and the interest is still contingent.

Answer to Problem 3-10
Step 1. The perpetuities period does not start until *O* dies, when the trust becomes irrevocable. At that time, *O*'s first child was born and ascertained (*C1*). The contingency is that *C1* must marry.

Step 2. *C1* can marry only during his lifetime; *C1* is the tentative measuring life.

Step 3. *C1* was in being. (The time when he must be in being is at *O*'s death.) The interest is valid.

Answer to Problem 3-11
Step 1. The perpetuities period starts at the time of the conveyance, since it is irrevocable.

Contingency #1: *O*'s first child must be born.
Contingency #2: He must marry.

Step 2.
Contingency #1. The child's parent, *O*, is the tentative measuring live.
Contingency #2. *O*'s first child can marry only during his lifetime; he is the tentative measuring life.

Step 3.
Contingency #1. *O* was in being.
Contingency #2. At the time of the conveyance, *O* had not had any children. His first child was not in being.

There is a measuring life for one of the contingencies but not for the other. The interest is invalid.

Step 4. The following events could occur:
1. After the conveyance, *O* has a child (as, indeed, happened: *C1*).
2. Everyone who was alive when the interest was created dies.
3. Twenty-one years later, *C1* is still alive and unmarried, but he could still marry. The interest is still contingent.

Answer to Problem 3-12

Step 1. The perpetuities period does not start until *O* dies, when his will takes effect. At that time, *O*'s first child was born and ascertained (it was *C1*). The contingency is that *C1* must marry.

Step 2. *C1* can marry only during his lifetime; *C1* is the tentative measuring life.

Step 3. *C1* was in being. (The time when he must be in being is at *O*'s death.) The interest is valid.

Answer to Problem 3-13
Step 1.
Contingency #1: *A*'s first child must be born.
Contingency #2: *A*'s first child must reach 21.

Step 2.
Contingency #1. *A* is the tentative measuring life.
Contingency #2. *A*'s first child will reach 21, if at all, sometime during his lifetime: he is a tentative measuring life. Also, *A* is a tentative measuring life: the latest that a child of *A* can reach 21 is 21 years after *A*'s death.

Step 3.
Contingency #1. *A* was in being.
Contingency #2. *A*'s first child was not in being, but *A* was.

We have found a measuring life for both contingencies (*A* works for both). The interest is valid.

Answer to Problem 3-14

Step 1. A grandchild of T must reach 25 after T's death. Note that that grandchild will not necessarily be $G1$. (Compare with "to the first grandchild of his, if he reaches 25 after T's death." Then, $G1$ is T's first grandchild, and only $G1$ could take.)

Step 2. All of T's grandchildren are the tentative measuring lives.

The parents of T's grandchildren are not tentative measuring lives because a grandchild can reach 25 more than 21 years after the death of the parent.

Step 3. T's children are alive, so more grandchildren of T can be born. T's grandchildren are not necessarily all in being. The interest is invalid.

Step 4. The following events could occur:
1. $G1$ dies.[30]
2. T's child $C1$ has a child, $G2$.
3. Everyone else who was alive when the interest was created dies.
4. Twenty-one years later, $G2$ is 21, he has not yet reached 25, and he might still reach 25. If he reaches 25, he will be T's first grandchild to reach 25 after T's death. The interest is still contingent.

Answer to Problem 3-15

Interest in A's first child
Step 1. A child of A must be born.

Step 2. A is the tentative measuring life. Since it is a life estate, which will *fail* at the death of the life tenant, A's first child is a tentative measuring life also.

Step 3. A was in being. (A's first child was not in being, but we only need one measuring life.) The interest is valid.

Interest in B's first child
Step 1. B's first child must be born.

Step 2. B is the tentative measuring life.

Step 3. B was in being. The interest is valid.

Answer to Problem 3-16

Step 1. A grandchild of A must reach 21. (Note that the first grandchild of A who reaches 21 is not necessarily $G1$; it could be *any one* of A's grandchildren, born or unborn.)

---

[30]This is not strictly necessary, because otherwise $G1$ would die in event #3. Since he is so close to satisfying the age contingency, however, the counterexample is more easily constructed by getting him out of the way at the outset.

Step 2. The grandchildren's parents are tentative measuring lives: all of *A*'s children, born and unborn.

A's grandchildren can reach 21 only during their lives. Therefore, all of *A*'s grandchildren, born and unborn, are also tentative measuring lives.

Step 3. Since *A* is alive, he can have more children, and *A*'s children are not necessarily all in being.

Since *A* is alive, he can have more children and more grandchildren, so *A*'s grandchildren are not necessarily all in being. The interest is invalid.

Step 4. The following events could occur:
1. *G1* dies.[31]
2. *A* has another child, *C1*.
3. Everyone in the world who was alive when the interest was created dies.
4. Twenty-one years later, *C1* can still have a child. If that child reaches 21, he will be the first grandchild of *A* who reaches 21. There is still a contingent interest in "the first grandchild of *A* who reaches 21."

Answer to Problem 3-17

Step 1. A grandchild of *A* must reach 21. (Note that the first grandchild of *A* who reaches 21 is not necessarily *G1*; it could be *any one* of *A*'s grandchildren, born or unborn.)

Step 2. The tentative measuring lives are the parents of *A*'s grandchildren, *i.e.*, all of *A*'s children.

A's grandchildren can reach 21 only during their lives. Therefore, all of *A*'s grandchildren, born and unborn, are also tentative measuring lives.

Step 3. Since *A* is dead, he cannot have more children, and all of *A*'s children were in being. They can serve as measuring lives. The interest is valid. (It is true that *C2* died before the conveyance, and in that sense one of *A*'s children is *not* in being. But this does not affect the analysis. By "in being" we mean that no other children can be born. The fact that one child is already dead does not prevent those who are alive from serving as the measuring lives.

A's grandchildren are not necessarily all in being, but that is unimportant, as we already have *A*'s children as the measuring lives.

Answer to Problem 3-18
Step 1.
Contingency #1. A grandchild of *O* must be born.
Contingency #2. That grandchild must reach 21.

---

[31]This is not strictly necessary, since he would die anyway as part of event #3. Since he is so near to satisfying the age contingency, however, we have one less thing to think about if we get rid of him right away.

Step 2.

Contingency #1. The parents, all of *O*'s children, are the tentative measuring lives.

Contingency #2. The latest time a grandchild of *O* can reach 21 is 21 years after the deaths of all of *O*'s children. All of *O*'s children are the tentative measuring lives for this contingency also. *O*'s first grandchild must reach 21, if at all, during his own lifetime, so the first grandchild himself is a tentative measuring life.

Step 3. Since this is a bequest and does not take effect until *O*'s death, all his children were in being. The interest is valid. (*O*'s first grandchild was not in being, but we already have a measuring life.)

Answer to Problem 3-19
Interest in A's first grandchild
Step 1. *A*'s first grandchild must be born.

Step 2. The tentative measuring lives are the parents of *A*'s first grandchild, *i.e.*, all of *A*'s children.

Since it is a life estate, the interest will *fail* at the death of the life tenant (one of the alternative ways of failing). So *A*'s first grandchild is a tentative measuring life.

Step 3. Since *A* was alive, his children were not necessarily all in being.
A's first grandchild was not in being either. The interest is invalid.

Step 4. The following events could occur:
1. *A* has another child, *C1*.
2. Everyone in the world who was alive when the interest was created dies.
3. Twenty-one years later, *C1* is still alive, he has not had any children, and he can still have a child (who would be *A*'s first grandchild). There is still a contingent interest in *A*'s first grandchild.

Interest in B
It is vested and valid.

Chapter 4
Applying the Rule to class gifts

The Rule against Perpetuities applies in a special way to class gifts. We precede our discussion of how class gifts are treated under the Rule with a review of the general law of class gifts. Our review is concise and omits some details; for more help, consult your casebook or other materials.

§ 4.01 Review of class gifts

[A] Introduction

So far we have dealt with instruments in which each interest was given to a single person. In the conveyance "to A for life, then to B," for example, only one person is named to take the life estate, and only one person is named to take the remainder in fee. A transferor could, instead, designate a number of persons to take the same interest. When that occurs, we could view what the transferor has done in either one of two ways, depending on the specific language he has used and other facts.

1. Individual gifts
We might conclude that the transferor has made *several individual* gifts; that is, he has created a separate interest in each one of the persons named as transferees. For example, the conveyance "to X for life, then to A, B, and C," would probably be interpreted in this way. That would mean that each of A, B, and C would own a 1/3 interest in the remainder. Their interests would be identical to the interests created by a conveyance "to X for life, then 1/3 to A, 1/3 to B, and 1/3 to C." (Note that each grantee will be a tenant in common with the others.)

2. Class gift
The alternative is to conclude that the transferor has given *one* interest to a *group* of persons. In that case, we would say that the transferor has made a "class gift." If, for example, the transferor had conveyed "to X for life, then to X's children," we would probably adopt this interpretation. We would then say that the remaindermen are the "group" or "class" of X's children, rather than the individual children of X. (Here also, those children of X who eventually come into possession or enjoyment of the property would take as tenants in common.)[1]

Which of these interpretations--individual gifts or class gift--is the "correct" one in a particular case depends on the language that the transferor used and, perhaps, the circumstances surrounding the transferor when the instrument was made.

---

[1]The two alternatives we have given are not the only possibilities. A gift could be partly a gift to a class and partly a gift to one or more individuals. For example, a gift to "X and the children of Y" could be either one class gift or, more likely, an individual gift to X and a class gift to the children of Y. Also, the interest may be a gift to "subclasses" (see § 4.04[A]).

We have not yet said what difference it makes whether we interpret an interest as a number of individual gifts or as one class gift. There *are* differences in the legal consequences which result from adopting one interpretation or the other. Those differences are the subject of section [B], which follows. In section [C], we discuss how to decide whether the transferor has created individual gifts or a class gift. In section [D], we discuss the "class-closing" rules.

Throughout our discussion of class gifts, we shall assume that any transfer of the type "to *A*, *B*, and *C*," creates three individual gifts, while a transfer of the type "to *X*'s children" creates a class gift.

[B] Consequences of classifying an interest as several individual gifts or as a class gift

[1] Death of will beneficiary before the testator

Individual gift
If an individual gift is created by a will, and the transferee dies before the testator, the individual gift fails (unless the anti-lapse statute applies). That is because the will does not become effective until the testator dies, and the will cannot create an interest in a nonexistent (in this case, dead) person. Therefore, the interest will pass to the testator's residuary beneficiaries or the testator's heirs instead.

> **Example 4-1**
> *T* devises Blackacre "to *A*, *B*, and *C*."
>
> Facts: *A* predeceased the testator, and the anti-lapse statute does not apply to *A*'s gift.

Remember that we are assuming that language of this sort creates individual gifts. The result is that *B* takes a 1/3 share, *C* takes a 1/3 share, and *A*'s 1/3 share goes to the persons named in the residuary clause of *T*'s will or, in the absence of a residuary clause, to *T*'s heirs. (Similarly, if *T* revokes *A*'s gift, it will fall into the residue or go to *T*'s heirs, and *B* and *C* will each take a 1/3 share.[2])

Class gift
If a class gift is created by will, and one of the members of the class dies before the testator, there is no reason for the gift to fail. Because the testator is making one gift to the "group" rather than individual gifts to individual persons, the *entire* gift is shared by whoever is in the group at the testator's death. That means that if there is at least one class member who is alive at the testator's death (and who has satisfied any conditions precedent), the gift will not fail. (Alternatively, the anti-lapse statute might apply.)

---

[2]L. Simes and A. Smith, The Law of Future Interests § 613, at 50 (2d ed. 1956).

Example 4-2
T devises Blackacre "to *X*'s children."

Facts: *X* had three children, *A*, *B*, and *C*, at the time the will was executed. Then *A* predeceased *T*, and the anti-lapse statute does not apply to *A*'s gift.

The result is that Blackacre is shared by *B* and *C*. (Children of *X* born after *T*'s death do not take because of the class-closing rules; see § 4.01[D].) Each of *B* and *C* takes a 1/2 interest as a tenant in common. (Similarly, if *T* *revokes* *A*'s share, *B* and *C* would each take a 1/2 interest.[3])

[2] Failure of a transferee to satisfy a condition

Individual gift

If an individual gift is subject to a condition precedent and the condition is not satisfied, then the gift fails, of course. If there is no alternative or succeeding interest, then enjoyment or possession of the property returns to the transferor, or to the transferor's heirs or residuary beneficiaries if the transferor has died.

Example 4-3
O conveys to *L* for life, then to *L*'s first child if that child survives *L*.

Facts: *L* has not had any children.

The remainder is an individual gift, because there will be only one person, at most, who meets the description. If *L* has a child and that child does not survive *L*, or if *L* never has any children, then the remainder fails. Since *O* did not state who is entitled to the property under those circumstances, *O* retained a reversion, and *O* will be entitled to possession upon *L*'s death.

Example 4-4
O conveys "to *L* for life, then to *L*'s children, *A*, *B*, and *C*, if they survive *L*."

Assuming that this creates an individual gift in each of *A*, *B*, and *C*, the result is very similar to that in the preceding example. If one of *L*'s children, say *A*, does not survive *L*, then his 1/3 interest in the remainder fails. Again, *O* has kept a reversion, and upon *L*'s death *O* will be entitled to a 1/3 interest in the property. He will be a tenant in common with *B* and *C*.

---

[3] *Id.*

Class gift

Example 4-5
O conveys "to *L* for life, then to such of *L*'s children as survive him."

Facts: *L* has three children, *A*, *B*, and *C*. *A* predeceased *L*.

There is a class gift in *L*'s children. When *A* died before *L*, *A*'s share in the class gift did *not* "fail." Rather, the entire gift of the remainder is to the *group* of "such of *L*'s children as survive him." The persons who are in that group (and we cannot determine who they are until *L* dies) take the *entire* interest. Therefore, upon *L*'s death, *B* and *C* will be entitled to the property, each with a 1/2 interest. *O* takes nothing.

It is not a good idea to say that *A*'s share in the class gift "went" to the other class members when *A* died during *L*'s lifetime. No interest actually passed from *A* to the others.

Of course, if *none* of *L*'s children survives him, the whole class gift fails, and *O* would be entitled to the property at *L*'s death.

No implied condition of survivorship
Note carefully one way in which individual gifts and class gifts do *not* differ. We noted earlier (§ 2.07) that there is no implied condition of survivorship for future interests. In "to *A* for life, then to *B*," for example, if *B* dies before *A*, the remainder will not fail but will pass to *B*'s heirs or will beneficiaries. The rule is the same for most future interests which are class gifts, as the following example illustrates.

Example 4-6
T makes a bequest "to *L* for life, then to *L*'s children."

Facts: At *T*'s death, *L* had three children, *A*, *B*, and *C*. *A* predeceased *L*.

Note the difference between this example and Example 4-5: here, there is no condition that the children survive *L*, so *A*'s death has no effect on his interest. Nor is this a case of a class member predeceasing the testator who made the class gift, as in Example 4-2. At *A*'s death he owned an interest which remained fully in existence afterwards, and it passed to his heirs or will beneficiaries. At *L*'s death, the property will be shared by *B*, *C*, and *A*'s successors.

However, a condition of survivorship is commonly implied in certain kinds of class gifts, *e.g.*, in a gift to issue. If *O* conveys "to *X* for life, then to *X*'s issue," *X*'s issue probably must survive him to take.

[3] Increase in the number of transferees

<u>Individual gift</u>.
Obviously, the number of transferees cannot increase as time passes. If only *A*, *B*, and *C* are named as transferees, then only they can take.

<u>Class gift</u>
A class gift is, by definition, a gift to a group of persons, and if the group is capable of increasing over time, then the number of transferees may increase. For example, if a gift is made "to *X* for life, then to *X*'s children," more children can be born as long as *X* is alive. As each child is born, the number of transferees (*i.e.*, class members) increases, while the share of each class member decreases. We say that the remainder in each existing child of *X* is "vested subject to partial divestment" or "vested subject to open" (§ 2.04[C][2]).

Note that *some* class gifts are *not* subject to an increase in the number of transferees. In "to *X* for life, then to *Y*'s children," the class membership would be fixed if *Y* was dead. But it is still appropriate to call the interest in *Y*'s children a class gift. For example, if this was a bequest, and one of *Y*'s children predeceased the testator, that child's share would not fall into the residue but would instead "go" to the other class members (assuming that the anti-lapse statute did not apply).

[C] Determining whether an interest constitutes individual gifts or a class gift

How do we decide whether an interest created in more than one person constitutes several individual gifts or one class gift? Not surprisingly, that determination is made by reference to the transferor's intent, and the language of the instrument is usually the best indicator of that intent. If the transferor used a group name without naming individual beneficiaries (for example, "to *X*'s children"), then we will almost certainly classify the interest as a class gift. If individual beneficiaries are named, we almost certainly have several individual gifts. Where the language is more ambiguous, we must discover the transferor's intent, elsewhere in the instrument or outside the instrument. We might ask whether the transferor was "group-minded": did he view the transferees as a "group" or as a number of individuals? Or, we can ask simply which legal consequences the transferor intended. For example, if the gift is by will and a beneficiary died before the testator, we might ask whether the testator intended the share of the predeceasing beneficiary to "go" to the other beneficiaries (in which case the gift would be a class gift) or to pass according to the residuary clause (in which case it would be a series of individual gifts).

[D] The class-closing rules

[1] The rule of convenience

We have noted that, if an interest is a class gift, then the number of persons who can share in that interest may increase over time. However, the number of persons who can share in a class gift will not increase forever. A class is said to "close" when persons who have not yet been born are precluded from sharing in the class gift.[4] A class can close in either of two ways.

First, a class can close biologically. In a gift to "*A*'s children," the class membership cannot increase once *A* is dead, and the class closes then at the latest. To say that a class closes under these circumstances is simply another way to say that an interest in an unborn person *fails* when his birth becomes impossible.

Second, the class may be closed *before* it is closed biologically by the "rule of convenience." Unless there is evidence of a contrary intent, the rule of convenience closes a class *as soon as a class member (or another in his place) is entitled to distribution of his share.*

We say "distribution of his share" here because most class gifts today are interests under a trust. If the class member has a legal future interest in land, then we would refer instead to the time when a class member is entitled to possession of the land.

We already know, from our discussion of contingent interests, what must happen before a class member is entitled to distribution of his share. He must be born and ascertained, any conditions precedent must be satisfied, and any preceding estates must terminate.

Notice that we said that the class closes when *a class member or another in his place* is entitled to distribution of his share. There are *three* sorts of persons who can demand distribution of a share in a class gift, once the requirements of the preceding paragraph are met:

1. If a class member is alive, he can demand distribution. (See Example 4-7, below.)

2. If a class member survives the testator (for a gift by will), but the class member dies before the time for distribution, and his interest does not fail at his death (it *would* fail, for example, if he does not satisfy a condition of survivorship), then his interest passes to his heirs or will beneficiaries.[5] Then *they* will be entitled to distribution. (See Example 4-8, below.)

---

[4]In the case of adopted persons, we would say that no person *adopted* after the class has closed can share in the class gift.

Also, a child who has been conceived is treated as if he has already been born. We will continue to say that the closing of the class excludes anyone not yet "born," but we actually mean that anyone not yet conceived is excluded.

[5]Remember that most class gifts are not subject to any *implied* condition of survival; see § 4.01[B][2].)

3. If the class gift was by will, and a class member predeceased the testator, and the anti-lapse statute applies,[6] then the class member's issue who survived the testator take his share. Those issue (or *their* heirs or will beneficiaries[7]) will be able to demand distribution of the class member's share. (See Example 4-9, below.)

Example 4-7
T makes a bequest in trust, income to *A* for life, then principal to *B*'s children.

Facts: *C1*, a child of *B*, was alive at *A*'s death.

There is a class gift in *B*'s children. At *A*'s death, *C1* is entitled to distribution of all or part the principal. Under the rule of convenience, the class will close then. That means that any child of *B* born after that time will not be entitled to take.

Example 4-8
T makes a bequest in trust, income to *A* for life, then principal to *B*'s children.

Facts: *C1*, a child of *B*, was alive at *T*'s death but predeceased *A*.

When *C1* died, his heirs or will beneficiaries succeeded to his interest, and upon *A*'s death *they* will be entitled to distribution of part or all of the principal. The class will close at *A*'s death.

Example 4-9
T makes a bequest in trust, income to *A* for life, then principal to *B*'s children.

Facts: *B*'s child *C1* predeceased *T*, leaving a child, *G1*, who survived *T*.

Assuming that the anti-lapse statute applies to *B*'s children, *G1* takes *C1*'s share. He will be entitled to distribution at *A*'s death, and the class will close then. If *G1* predeceases *A*, *G1*'s heirs or will beneficiaries succeed to his interest (just as *C1*'s heirs or will beneficiaries succeeded to his interest in Example 4-8), and they will be entitled to distribution at *A*'s death, closing the class at that time.

---

[6]The anti-lapse statute might not apply because the class member was not in the degree of relationship to the testator which the statute requires, or the statute might not apply to class gifts.

[7]One of the issue might survive the testator but die before distribution.

The rule of convenience is only a rule of construction, not a rule of law. If there is evidence that the transferor wanted the number of persons sharing in the class gift to continue to increase after the time when the rule of convenience would close the class, then the rule of convenience will not apply.

Application of the rule of convenience is trickier when the class gift is subject to a condition precedent, as in the next example.

Example 4-10
To *A* for life, then to such of *B*'s children as attain the age of 21.

A child of *B* will be able to demand distribution of part of the principal only if *A* is dead *and* that child has reached 21. Only when both those facts are true will the class close. (If a child reaches 21 and then dies, his heirs or will beneficiaries will be able to demand distribution at *A*'s death.)

The closing of the class prevents only those persons who *have not yet been born* from taking a share. Any person who is already born but has not yet satisfied the condition precedent can still take a share, once he satisfies the condition. In Example 4-10, once the class closes, any child of *B* who has already been born but who has not yet reached 21 will share in the class gift, if and when he reaches 21.

Point of potential confusion

Sometimes it is said that closing the class means that no one else can "enter" the class. This is a dangerous way of expressing the class closing rule, because it requires you to be very careful in defining the "class" that persons are prevented from "entering." The preceding example illustrates the point. In that example, there is a tendency to mistakenly think of the "class" as consisting of "all of *B*'s children who have reached 21." Then, if we say that closing the class means that no one can "enter" the class, we would conclude that any child of B *who was not yet 21 when the class closed* would be excluded from any share in the gift. But that is *not* the result. As we have seen, children of *B* who reach 21 after the class has closed *are* entitled to share in the gift; it is only children *born* (or adopted) after the class has closed who cannot take.

The class ought really to be described as "all of *B*'s children"; the requirement of reaching 21 is a condition precedent attached to the class gift. If we think of the class in that way, then it *is* true that no one can "enter" the class of "*B*'s children" after it has closed.

You can avoid this potential for error by thinking of the class closing rule in the way we described it earlier, without using the concept of "entering" the class: no one born after the class has closed can take a share in the class gift.

It is possible for a class to close immediately.

Example 4-11
T bequeaths $1000 to "*A*'s children."

Facts: *T* is survived by *A* and *A*'s first child, *C1*.

C1 is born and ascertained, and there is no condition precedent which must be satisfied. Nor is there a preceding estate which must end before *C1* is entitled to distribution. *C1* is entitled to distribution at *T*'s death, and the class closes. *C1* takes the entire gift; children born to *A* after *T*'s death do not take a share.

[2] In a gift of income, the class "closes" separately for each payment

Example 4-12
Income to *A*'s children for their lives.

Facts: *A* has one child, *C1*.

At first, *A*'s sole child, *C1*, receives all the income. But the fact that *C1* is entitled to all of the income does *not* close the class under the rule of convenience. If another child, *C2*, is born, he receives 1/2 of the income and *C1* receives 1/2. There is no inconvenience in leaving the class open, because the payment of income is periodic. Similarly, if a third child is born, each child will receive a 1/3 share, and so on.

[3] If no class member has been born by the time distribution might otherwise take place, the class does not close until it is biologically closed[8]

Example 4-13
T makes a devise to *A*'s children.

Facts: *A* has his first child, *C1*, one year after *T*'s death.

Because no child of *A* had been born by the time of *T*'s death, the rule of convenience does *not* close the class when *C1* is born. The class remains open until it is biologically closed at *A*'s death, and all of *A*'s children whenever born will share in the gift. In this case, that means that *C1* receives the property but holds it subject to partial divestment by the birth of more children.[9]

---

[8]Except for per capita class gifts; see section [4] below.

[9]5 American Law of Property § 22.42 at 355 (A. Casner ed. 1952).

The result is justified on the basis of the testator's presumed intent. If the class were to close at T's death, no child of A would be entitled to take, and the gift would be entirely ineffective. The testator could not have intended such a result. It seems harder to justify waiting beyond CI's birth to close the class, but it has been said that letting in one afterborn child (CI) and not others would be irrational. The testator is thought to intend, under these circumstances, that all of A's children, whenever born, be entitled to take.[10]

Example 4-14
T makes a devise to L for life, then to A's children.

Facts: A has his first child, CI, one year after L's death.

Because no child of A had been born by L's death (when distribution would otherwise occur), the rule of convenience does *not* close the class when CI is born. The class remains open until it is biologically closed at A's death, and all of A's children whenever born will share in the gift.[11]

[4] Class closing rule for a per capita class gift

So far in our discussion of class gifts, we have been speaking of one gift to be divided among the members of the class. However, a testator can instead give a *specified sum* to *each* member of the class. In that case, the class closes at the testator's death, even if no class member is entitled to take then.

Example 4-15
T bequeaths $100 to each child of A.

---

[10]5 American Law of Property § 22.42 at 355-356 (A. Casner ed. 1952); L. Simes and A. Smith, The Law of Future Interests § 636 at 73, 74 (2d ed. 1956).

[11]Things get trickier when there is a condition precedent. Suppose T makes a devise to A's children who reach 21. If at T's death no child of A has been born, then the rule appears to be that the class does not close until it is biologically closed at A's death. If at T's death a child of A has been born but no child of A has reached 21, then the rule of convenience *will* apply: the class will close when a child of A reaches 21. 5 American Law of Property § 22.44, at 377 (A. Casner ed. 1952); L. Simes, Handbook of the Law of Future Interests 210 (1966).

Finally, suppose T makes a devise to L for life, then to A's children who reach 21. At least one case holds that if no child of A has been *born* by the time L's life estate ends, then the class will remain open until it is biologically closed at A's death. *Conduitt v. Soane*, 4 Jur. (N.S.) 502 (Ch. 1858); 5 American Law of Property § 22.45, at 386 (A. Casner ed. 1952).

This is a per capita class gift. In order that the rest of T's estate be distributed to the other beneficiaries, we have to know at T's death how much to set aside for the children of A. Therefore, the class closes at T's death regardless of whether there are then any persons who can demand distribution. If a child of A is in existence at the time of T's death, the class will close then, as in the case of a class gift that is not per capita. But even if no children of A have been born by the time of T's death, the class will close at T's death; in that case the gift fails entirely. This result is different from that for a class gift which is not per capita (see Example 4-13).

Similarly, if the testator makes a per capita class gift which is subject to a condition precedent, and no class member has satisfied the condition at the testator's death, still the class closes at his death, in order to make possible the distribution of the rest of his estate.

§ 4.02 Application of the Rule

The Rule applies to class gifts in a special manner. There are various ways to describe how the Rule applies to class gifts, but the description which is easiest to understand and apply is the following.

> If the interest of *any* class member is bad under the Rule, the interests of *all* class members are bad.

This is called the "all or nothing" rule. It is subject to two exceptions which we discuss later.

Another way of describing how the Rule against Perpetuities applies to class gifts is to say that the size of the share of each class member must be determined within the perpetuities period.[12] For most purposes, however, the "all or nothing" formula is easier to work with.

The application of the Rule to class gifts is illustrated by the following examples.

Example 4-16
O makes a bequest in trust to pay the income to A for his life, then to pay the income to A's children for their lives, and upon the death of the last surviving child to pay the principal to A's grandchildren.[13]

Facts: A has one child, $C1$, and one grandchild, $G1$.

---

[12]This is not required of life estates, because of "implied cross-remainders." See § 4.05.

[13]We assume, in this and other examples, that the grandchildren take per capita and not per stirpes. A per stirpes distribution *might* result in a distribution to "subclasses," and the all-or-nothing rule would not apply to all grandchildren. See § 4.04[A].

We evaluate the grandchildren's interest by applying the familiar four-step procedure, as follows.[14]

Step 1 (state the contingencies): The interest of $G1$ is a vested remainder subject to partial divestment and is not subject to the Rule except as the all-or-nothing principle may affect it. There is a contingent interest in all unborn grandchildren. The contingency for their interest is that they must be born.

Step 2 (find the tentative measuring lives): The only persons whose deaths will resolve the contingency that more grandchildren must be born are the parents of those grandchildren, i.e., all of A's children. The interest in A's grandchildren is not limited to children of $C1$, so we must describe the tentative measuring lives as all of A's children, including potential future (unborn) children of A.

Step 3 (in being?): A is alive, so "all of A's children" are not necessarily in being. Therefore, the interest is invalid.

Step 4 (construct a counterexample): The following events could occur:

1. After T's death, another child, $C2$, is born to A. (Note that $C2$ was not alive when the interest was created, so he cannot be a measuring life himself.)

2. Everyone in the world who was alive when the interest was created dies, and the 21-year timer starts to run.

3. Twenty-one years later the timer rings. $C2$ is still alive, he could still have a child (who would be a grandchild of A), and therefore there is still a contingent interest in A's (unborn) grandchildren.

The contingent interest in unborn grandchildren is bad. This means, under the all-or-nothing rule, that *the interest in G1*, the grandchild who was alive at the creation of the interest, is bad, even though he had a vested remainder (subject to partial divestment).

You can see that there is nothing greatly different about the *basic* application of the Rule to class gifts. We still have to identify contingencies and find tentative measuring lives, and we do so in the same way we performed those tasks in connection with individual gifts. The important things to remember are (1) the existence of a contingent interest in unborn class members (as long as the class has not closed) and (2) the operation of the all-or-nothing principle in striking interests in class members whose interests otherwise look valid.

---

[14]We discuss how the children's interest is evaluated under the Rule in § 4.05.

§ 4.03 Using the class-closing rule to help validate an interest

When we were learning how to apply the Rule to individual gifts, we saw that two common contingencies are resolved at the deaths of the *parents* of transferees. First, a contingency that a child must be born is resolved at the deaths of that child's (potential) parents (Fact #2, § 3.07[C]), and we select the parents as tentative measuring lives in Step 2 of the four-step procedure. (We are using "child" in the widest possible sense here. He could be a child of the transferor, a child of the transferor's child (i.e., a grandchild of the transferor), or a child of any other person.) Second, a contingency that a child must reach the age of 21 (or less) is also resolved at the death of the child's (potential) parents (Fact #3), and we select the parents as tentative measuring lives for that contingency as well. *The reason that the parents work as tentative measuring lives for these two contingencies is this: at the parents' deaths, no more children can be born, and any contingent interest in unborn children fails.*

Class gifts, too, are often subject to these two contingencies, and the parents will be tentative measuring lives for the reasons we just mentioned. But with class gifts, there might be an additional way of resolving these contingencies. We know that when a class gift to children (again using "children" in the broad sense noted in the preceding paragraph) has closed under the rule of convenience, no unborn children can share in the class gift--in other words, any interest in unborn (potential) class members fails. Therefore, a person whose death will certainly cause the class to close under the rule of convenience (immediately or within 21 years) will work as another tentative measuring life. *The reason that a person whose death closes the class works as a tentative measuring life for the two contingencies described in the preceding paragraph is this: at his death, no unborn child can share in the class gift, and any contingent interest in unborn children fails.*

We might call the person whose death causes the class to close under the rule of convenience a "class-closing tentative measuring life."[15] Compare the italicized statements in the two preceding paragraphs. The parents close the class biologically; the class-closing tentative measuring life closes the class under the rule of convenience-- we might even think of him as an "artificial parent" for purposes of applying the four-step procedure.[16]

In summary:

> *If the parent of an unborn class member works as a tentative measuring life under Step 2, someone whose death closes the class under the rule of convenience (immediately or within 21 years) will also work as a tentative measuring life.*

---

[15]The parent closes the class also (biologically), but we reserve this term for a person who closes the class under the rule of convenience.

[16]In § 2.06[B] we referred to the closing of a class as an alternative way of failing. See also § 3.07[B], under "Alternative ways of failing."

Example 4-17
O conveys to *A* for life, then to *A*'s grandchildren.

Facts: *A* has one grandchild, *G1*.

Step 1 (state the contingencies): There is a contigent interest in unborn grandchildren of *A*; the contingency is that they must be born.

Step 2 (find the tentative measuring lives): That contingency will be resolved at the deaths of the parents of *A*'s grandchildren, that is, at the deaths of *A*'s children. "All of *A*'s children" are tentative measuring lives.

But there is *another* way of resolving the contingency that *A*'s grandchildren must be born. Once the class has closed, the contingent interest in unborn grandchildren *fails*, because unborn grandchildren will no longer be able to share in the class gift. Therefore, anyone whose death will surely cause the class to close under the rule of convenience,[17] immediately or within another 21 years, is another tentative measuring life.

Is there anyone whose death will surely cause the class to close? The class will close when one grandchild can demand distribution of his share; is there a time when that must happen? If *G1* is alive at *A*'s death, *G1* will be able to demand distribution of his share, and the class will close under the rule of convenience. If *G1* dies before *A*'s death, his interest will pass to his heirs or will beneficiaries, and *they* will be able to demand distribution of *G1*'s share at *A*'s death, so again the rule of convenience will close the class at that time. We are certain, then, that the class will close at *A*'s death. Therefore, *A* is another tentative measuring life, the "class-closing tentative measuring life."

Step 3 (in being?): "All of *A*'s children" are not necessarily in being, because *A* is still alive.

The other person identified in Step 2 as a tentative measuring life was *A*. *A* *was* in existence, so he qualifies as a measuring life. The interest is good.

Example 4-18
O conveys to *A* for life, then to *A*'s grandchildren.

Facts: *A* has never had any grandchildren.

The example is identical to Example 4-17 except for the facts that are given.

Step 1 (state the contingencies): The contingency is that the grandchildren must be born.

---

[17]The tentative measuring lives we have already chosen, all of *A*'s children, close the class biologically at their deaths.

Step 2 (find the tentative measuring lives): "All of *A*'s children" are tentative measuring lives.

Is there *another* way of resolving the contingency that *A*'s grandchildren must be born? *A* worked in the preceding example because *we were certain that* A*'s death would close the class*. In this example, if no grandchildren of *A* are born by the time of *A*'s death, the class will not close then under the rule of convenience. Instead, it will remain open until it is biologically closed at the deaths of all of *A*'s children (see Example 4-14). Because we cannot be *certain* that the class will close at *A*'s death (or within 21 years thereafter), *A* will *not* work as a class-closing tentative measuring life.

Step 3 (in being?): *A*'s children are not necessarily all in being. The interest is invalid.

Step 4 (construct a counterexample):

1. *A* has another child, *C1*. (It is immaterial whether or not this is *A*'s first child.)

2. Everyone in the world who was alive when the interest was created (including *A*) dies. The 21-year timer starts to run. Although *A* has died, the class does not close, because there was no class member who could demand his share. Therefore, the class must remain open until all of *A*'s children have died.

4. Twenty-one years later, *C1* is still alive, he can still have a child (a grandchild of *A*), who would be able to share in the class gift. There is still a contingent interest in unborn grandchildren.

> **Example 4-19**
> *O* conveys to *A* for life, then to *B*'s children who reach 25.
>
> Facts: *B* has a child, *C1*, aged 26.

Step 1 (state the contingencies): The interest in *C1* is not contingent; it is vested (subject to partial divestment). However, there is a contingent remainder in *B*'s unborn children:
Contingency #1: *B*'s children must be born.
Contingency #2: *B*'s children must reach 25.

Step 2 (find the tentative measuring lives):

Contingency #1. *B*'s death resolves this contingency (Fact #2, § 3.07[B]).

This is a class gift for which we have just selected the *parent* of unborn class members as the tentative measuring life for the first contingency. Therefore, we should also look for a class-closing tentative measuring life. Is there someone whose death will surely close the class, immediately or within 21 years? If *C1* is alive when *A* dies, *C1* will be able to demand distribution, since he has already satisfied the condition precedent of reaching 25. If *C1* is not alive when *A* dies, then *C1*'s interest passed upon his death to his heirs or will beneficiaries, and *they* will be able to demand distribution at *A*'s death. *A*'s death will surely close the class. Therefore, his death resolves the birth contingency, and he is another tentative measuring life.

Perhaps you see that in this example it was unnecessary to look for a class-closing tentative measuring life. Such a person works no better as a *tentative* measuring life than the parent himself. Therefore, the only way a class-closing tentative measuring life will help us is if he meets the *in-being requirement* and the parent does not. Here, *B* was in being and can serve as the actual measuring life for the first contingency, so we have nothing to gain by looking for another tentative measuring life. But there is little harm in doing so anyway.

Contingency #2. The deaths of all of *B*'s children resolve this contingency (Fact #1, § 3.07[B]), and they are tentative measuring lives. *B*'s death resolves the contingency within 25 years (Fact #3), but that is not soon enough for *B* to serve as a tentative measuring life. Because the parent, *B*, does not work as a tentative measuring life, a class-closing tentative measuring life will not work either, and there is no point in trying to find one.

Step 3 (in being?): As for contingency #1, both *A* and *B* are in being. As for contingency #2, however, *B* is alive, and all his children are not necessarily in being. We have not been able to find measuring lives for both contingencies, and the interest is invalid.

Step 4 (construct a counterexample):

1. *B* has another child, *C2*. (*C2* will be able to share in the class gift if he reaches 25, because the class has not yet closed.)
2. Immediately afterward, everyone in the world who was alive when the interest was created dies (this includes *A*). (Now the class closes, because *C1*'s heirs or will beneficiaries can demand distribution of his share, but the closing of the class at this time is not important for purposes of the counterexample.)
3. Twenty-one years later, *C2* is 21 years old, and the contingency that he must reach 25 is still unresolved.

Because there is still a contingent interest in *C2* under these circumstances, his interest (*i.e.*, the interest in all unborn children of *B*) is bad under the Rule, and-- under the all-or-nothing rule--the interest of *C1* is bad as well.

Example 4-20
O conveys to *A* for life, then to *B*'s grandchildren who reach 21.

Facts: *B* has had only one grandchild, *G1*, who is now 22 years old.

Step 1 (state the contingencies): The unborn grandchildren have a contingent interest:

Contingency #1: They must be born.
Contingency #2: They must reach 21.

Step 2 (find the tentative measuring lives). As for contingency #1, the unborn class members' parents, all of *B*'s children, are the tentative measuring lives. As for the second contingency, *B*'s children are also the tentative measuring lives (Fact #3, § 3.07[B]). *B*'s grandchildren themselves are also tentative measuring lives for the second contingency.

Since we have selected the *parents* of the class members as the tentative measuring lives, we should look for a class-closing tentative measuring life as well. *G1* has already satisfied the condition precedent. Therefore, it is certain that he, or his heirs or will beneficiaries if he predeceases *A*, will be able to demand distribution of a share at *A*'s death. The class will surely close at *A*'s death. Since the parents of the unborn class members worked as tentative measuring lives for both contingencies, *A* will work as a class-closing tentative measuring life for both contingencies as well.

Step 3 (in being?): Since *B* was alive, *B*'s children were not necessarily all in being. They do not work as measuring lives. *B*'s grandchildren were not necessarily all in being and do not work as measuring lives either. Our other tentative measuring life for both contingencies, *A*, *was* in being. The interest is good.

We can state our analysis in a slightly different way which you might find helpful. The latest possible time that the class will close is at *A*'s death. (It would close earlier if *B* and all of *B*'s children died before *A*'s death.) Therefore, the *latest possible time* that a class member (*i.e.*, a grandchild who has the possibility of taking a share) could be born is immediately before *A*'s death,[18] and the *latest possible time* that a class member will reach 21 is 21 years after *A*'s death. *A* works as a measuring life.

A person will work as a "class-closing tentative measuring life" only if we are *certain* that his death will close the class, immediately or within 21 years. The following example, which is identical to the preceding one except for the facts, illustrates this point.

Example 4-21
O conveys to *A* for life, then to *B*'s grandchildren who reach 21.

Facts: *B* has had only one grandchild, *G1*, who is now 20 years old.

The analysis begins as our earlier one did:

Step 1 (state the contingencies): The unborn grandchildren have a contingent interest:

Contingency #1: They must be born.

---

[18] A class member could be born after *A*'s death if he had been conceived at the time of *A*'s death, but that does not change the analysis.

Contingency #2: They must reach 21.

Step 2 (find the tentative measuring lives). As for contingency #1, the unborn class members' parents, all of B's children, are the tentative measuring lives. As for the second contingency, B's children are also the tentative measuring lives (Fact #3). B's grandchildren themselves are also tentative measuring lives for the second contingency.

Since we have selected the *parents* of the class members as the tentative measuring lives, we should look for a class-closing tentative measuring life as well. Here the analysis diverges from our previous discussion. The class will close at A's death only if there is someone then alive who can demand distribution of his share of the class gift. But we cannot be certain that that will be the case. $G1$ might die before he reaches 21. In that case his interest would fail (because he did not satisfy the condition precedent), and it would not pass to his heirs or will beneficiaries. There might be no other person who can demand distribution of a share at A's death. Since there is no certainty that the class will close at A's death, we cannot use him as a class-closing tentative measuring life.

Step 3 (in being?): Since B is alive, his children are not necessarily all in being. B's grandchildren are not all in being either. The interest is invalid.

Step 4 (construct a counterexample): The following could occur:
1. $G1$ dies.
2. B has another child, $C1$.
3. Everyone who was alive when the interest was created dies. This means that A dies, but no grandchild of B was 21 at A's death, so the class remains open.
4. Twenty-one years later, $C1$ is still alive, he could still have a child (B's grandchild) who reaches 21, and there is still a contingent interest in B's grandchildren.

The most difficult kind of class-gift problem involves a gift which is vested with enjoyment postponed.

Example 4-22
O makes a conveyance to A for life, then to the grandchildren of A, to be paid at their respective ages of 25.[19]

Facts: No grandchild of A has reached 25.

Step 1 (state the contingencies): Grandchildren of A must be born. There is no contingency that grandchildren reach age 25, because the age "condition" only postpones the time of payment (see § 2.04[C][1]).

---

[19]From 6 American Law of Property § 24.25, at 81 (A. Casner ed. 1952).

Step 2 (find the tentative measuring lives): Since there is a birth contingency, we choose the parents as the tentative measuring lives: all of *A*'s children. The grand-children themselves are also tentative measuring lives.

Since we have chosen *parents* as tentative measuring lives, we ought to look for a class-closing tentative measuring life. In order for *A* to work as a class-closing tentative measuring life, we must be *certain* that the class will close at *A*'s death or within 21 years thereafter. The class will close only if a grandchild can demand payment, and that will be true only if *a grandchild of* A *is 25 years old* or if *a grandchild who predeceased* A *would have been 25 years old had the grandchild lived*[20] (in addition to *A* being dead). Therefore, in order for *A* to work as a class-closing tentative measuring life, we must be *certain* that one of the two italicized facts will be true within 21 years after *A*'s death. But we cannot know how long *A* will live; he could die tomorrow. Therefore, we can be sure that one of the two italicized facts will be true within 21 years after *A*'s death only if we can be sure that one of them will be true within 21 years from *now*, the date of the conveyance. If a grandchild of *A* is 4 years old now, then either (1) he will reach the age of 25 within 21 years, or (2) he will die in the interim, but in that case he would have reached the age of 25 within 21 years. *A* will work as a class-closing tentative measuring life if a grandchild is at least 4 years old at the time of the conveyance.[21]

Step 3 (in being?): Neither *A*'s children nor *A*'s grandchildren work as measuring lives because they are not necessarily all in being. *A*, our other (possible) tentative measuring life, is in being. Referring to the conditions under which *A* works as a tentative measuring life, we can say that the interest is good if a grandchild is at least 4 years old at the time of the conveyance. (The interest would be good also if *A* is dead; then his children work as measuring lives.)

Step 4. If no grandchild of *A* is at least 4 years old, then we can construct a counterexample:

1. *A* has another child, *C1*.
2. Everyone who was alive at the time the interest was created dies.
3. Twenty-one years later, all grandchildren are still under 25 (because we assumed they were all under 4 at the time the interest was created). There fore, there is still no one who is entitled to payment, and the class remains open. If *C1* has a child, that child (a grandchild of *A*) will be a member of the class. There is still a contingent interest in unborn grandchildren of *A*.

§ 4.04 Exceptions to the all-or-nothing rule

There are two exceptions to the principle that if the interest of one class member is invalid under the Rule, then the interests of *all* class members are invalid.

---

[20]In the latter case, the grandchild's heirs or will beneficiaries are entitled to payment.

[21]It is not sufficient that a grandchild who was dead at the time of the conveyance would have been 4 years old had he lived. Such a person would not be a transferee.

[A] Gifts to subclasses

When we discussed the general law relating to class gifts, we started by supposing that the transferor has created an interest in more than one person. We saw that, depending on the facts, such an interest would be construed either as one gift to a group (a class gift) or several gifts to several different individuals (individual gifts). But there is another possibility: if there is more than one transferee, we might view the transferees as composing two or more groups. In other words, there is one gift to one group, a second gift to another group, and so on. What appears to be *one* gift to *one* class is really *several* gifts to *several* classes, which we call "subclasses."

The following example illustrates how we identify gifts to subclasses.

> **Example 4-23**
> *T* makes a bequest in trust, income to *L* for her life, then income to *L*'s children for their respective lives. Upon the death of each child of *L*, a share of the principal, proportionate to the share of income which that child had been receiving, shall be paid to that child's children.
>
> Facts: At *T*'s death, *L* had two children, *C1* and *C2*.

If we viewed all the grandchildren as a single large class taking one gift, then the interests of all the grandchildren would be bad. The contingency is that the grandchildren must be born, so *L*'s children are the tentative measuring lives. But since *L* is still alive, *L*'s children were not necessarily all in being when *T* died. Therefore, the interest would be bad in all grandchildren under the all-or-nothing rule.

But a correct interpretation of the instrument is that it creates not one gift to a single class but several gifts to subclasses. If it were one gift to a single class, the size of each class member's share would depend on how many class members there are. To review this notion, consider a gift to A for life, then to A's children, where A has a child *C1*. As more children are born, *C1*'s share decreases in size.

Now consider the gift in the Example. Suppose that *C1* has a child, *G1*, and *C2* has a child, *G2*. *C1* is entitled to one-half the income, so *G1* receives one-half the principal upon *C1*'s death. Similarly, *C2* is entitled to one-half the income, so *G2* receives one-half the principal upon *C2*'s death. If *C2* has another child, *G3*, then upon *C2*'s death one-half of the principal is distributed to *G2* and *G3*, so each of them takes a one-fourth share. Clearly the size of *G2*'s share in the principal is affected by the number of children *C2* has; all of *C2*'s children are in one subclass. But the birth of *G3* does not affect the size of *G1*'s share; he still receives one-half the principal upon *C1*'s death. This is simply a consequence of the way the trust is set up. Therefore, we say that the children of *C1* are in one subclass, the children of *C2* are in another subclass, and so on for children of other children that *L* may have.

How does the Rule apply to a gift to subclasses? First, the all-or-nothing principle applies only *within* each subclass, not to the whole gift (*i.e.*, not "across" subclasses). If the interest of one class member is bad, then the interests of transferees who are *in the same subclass* are also bad, under the all-or-nothing rule. But the interests of transferees who are members of a different subclass are not affected. We apply the Rule (and the all-or-nothing principle) separately to each subclass, in the same way that the Rule applies separately to each individual gift.

Second, when we evaluate the interest of each subclass, the size of the share to be divided among the members of that subclass must become fixed within the perpetuities period.[22]

> **Example 4-24**
> *T* makes a bequest in trust, income to *L* for her life, then income to *L*'s children for their respective lives. Upon the death of each child of *L*, a share of the principal, proportionate to the share of income which that child had been receiving, shall be paid to that child's children.
>
> Facts: At *T*'s death, *L* had two children, *C1* and *C2*. After *T*'s death, *L* had another child, *C3*.

This example is identical to the previous one, except that we have hypothesized the birth of another child, *C3*. First let us consider the interest in the children of *C3*. The contingency that those children must be born is resolved at the death of their parent, *C3*. *C3* was not in being and cannot serve as a measuring life. Therefore, the interest in children of *C3* is invalid. We have cheated a little for the sake of clarity. We probably should not refer to *C3* by name, because his birth is a fact that we cannot take into account, having occurred after the perpetuities period began. To speak more generally, we can say that the interests in the children of *any* child of *L* born after *T*'s death are invalid.

But the all-or-nothing rule applies only within each subclass. The invalidity of the interests in children of afterborn children of *L* does not affect the interests in children of *C1* or *C2*, and we turn next to them.

Looking first at the subclass of the children of *C1*, we see that the contingency that a child of *C1* must be born will be resolved at *C1*'s death. He is the tentative measuring life; since he was in being, he will work as an actual measuring life.

We are not quite done yet. The second requirement is that the size of the share for the whole subclass of *C1*'s children must become fixed within the perpetuities period. The size of the share for the subclass depends on the number of children that *L* has. That will be determined by the time of *L*'s death. Therefore, *L* is the tentative

---

[22]*American Security & Trust Co. v. Cramer*, 175 F.Supp. 367 (D.D.C. 1959); T. Bergin and P. Haskell, Preface to Estates in Land and Future Interests 195-196 (2d ed. 1984); L. Waggoner, Future Interests in a Nutshell 253 (1981).

Or, we could encompass both requirements by saying that the size of the share of each *member* of the subclass must be fixed within the perpetuities period (for fee interests).

measuring life for the second requirement. *L* was in being and works as an actual measuring life. The measuring lives for the interest in *C1*'s children are *C1* and *L*.

The interest in the children of *C2* would be valid under the same analysis.

In all our previous examples involving a remainder in fee in grandchildren, there was no division into subclasses because all the grandchildren took the entire property when the last child died. In those examples, we should assume also that the distribution to the grandchildren is per capita and not per stirpes; a per stirpes distribution *might* result in the creation of subclasses,[23] although that result appears incorrect.[24]

[B] Per capita gifts to a class

A per capita gift to a class (§ 4.01[D][4]) represents the second exception to the all-or-nothing rule. In a per capita gift, we apply the Rule as if there was an individual gift to each class member. In other words, each class member's gift is evaluated separately, and the all-or-nothing rule does not apply.

> **Example 4-25**
> *T* bequeaths "$1,000 to each of the children of *A*, including those children born after my death, who attain the age of thirty years."
>
> Facts: At *T*'s death, *A* is alive and has had two children, *C1* and *C2*, neither of whom has attained the age of thirty.

Because this is a per capita class gift, we evaluate the interest of each of *A*'s children separately. *C1*'s interest is subject only to the contingency that he reach 30. That will happen, if it all, during *C1*'s lifetime, so *C1* is the tentative measuring life, and *C1* was in being, so he can serve as the actual measuring life. The interest of *C2* is valid by the same analysis. Children of *A* who were not yet born at *T*'s death also apparently have an interest; it is contingent on their birth as well as on their reaching 30. However, there is no measuring life for the contingency of reaching 30, and the interest of such children is invalid. But the invalidity of their interest does *not* affect the interests of *C1* and *C2*, because the all-or-nothing rule does not apply to a per capita class gift.[25]

Suppose the bequest had not included the words "including those children born after my death." Because the testator has not expressed a contrary intent, the class closes at his death (see § 4.01[D][3]). That means that only those persons alive at *T*'s death can take, and they can serve as their own measuring lives. The interest is good.

---

[23]*Second Bank-State St. Trust Co. v. Second Bank-State St. Trust Co.*, 335 Mass. 407, 140 N.E.2d 201 (1957).

[24]6 American Law of Property § 24.29, at 90 n. 6a (A. Casner ed. 1952); L. Waggoner, Future Interests in a Nutshell 257-258 (1981).

[25]Simes & Smith, The Law of Future Interests § 1266, at 199 (2d ed. 1956).

A more complicated example is given as Problem 4-10, § 4.06.

§ 4.05 Life interests in more than one person

Consider the following example:

> **Example 4-26**
> *T* makes a bequest in trust, income to *A* for his life, then income to *A*'s children for their lives, and upon the death of the last surviving child principal to *A*'s grandchildren.
>
> Facts: *A* has no children.

We have discussed how the Rule applies to the interest in *A*'s grandchildren (and we have seen that it is void), but we have avoided discussing how the *children's* interest fares under the Rule. We now address that issue.

The language "income to *A*'s children for their lives" means that the income is split equally among the children alive from time to time. Then, when only one child remains alive, he receives the entire income until his death. At that time, the principal is distributed (in the example, to *T*'s residuary beneficiaries or heirs instead of the grandchildren, because their interest is invalid).

The interest in *A*'s children is valid under the Rule, but it is particularly easy to be misled into thinking that their interest is invalid. We shall first show *how you might be tricked into concluding, wrongly, that the interest in* A's *children is bad under the Rule.* Then we shall show why the interest is, in fact, good.

Suppose that *after T*'s bequest in the example, *A* has two children, *C1* and *C2*, and that both children are alive at *A*'s death. We know that each of *C1* and *C2* is entitled to 1/2 of the income while both of them are alive. If *C1* dies first, then *C2* will be entitled to an additional 1/2 of the income, *i.e.*, the share that *C1* had previously been receiving. If, on the other hand, *C2* dies first, then *C1* will be entitled to an additional 1/2 of the income, *i.e.*, the share that *C2* had previously been receiving. So it *appears* that each of the children has a contingent remainder in the "other" 1/2 of the income; the condition precedent is surviving the other child. The contingency of being the survivor will not be resolved until the death of one of the children, of course. The children cannot serve as measuring lives for that contingency because they were not in being. And *A* cannot serve as a tentative measuring life, because the death of one of *A*'s children will not necessarily occur within 21 years of *A*'s death. The interest in *A*'s children *appears* bad.

The reasoning just given is wrong because *A*'s children, once they are born, do not have a contingent remainder; there is no condition precedent. The language that the testator used in describing the children's interest is usually considered equivalent to the following (once both children are born and assuming that *A* had only 2 children):

1. Pay one-half of the income to *C1* for life,
   then to *C2* for life <-- ["cross-remainder"]

2. Pay one-half of the income to *C2* for life,
   then to *C1* for life <-- ["cross-remainder"]

The second life estate for each half-share of income is called a "cross-remainder." In this case, because the testator did not create the remainders explicitly, they are *implied* cross-remainders (for life).[26]

You can see what happens if, for example, *C1* dies first. His one-half share in the income under paragraph 1 ends, and *C2* begins to receive that income instead, by virtue of *C2*'s life estate under that paragraph. At the same time, *C2* continues to receive one-half the income under paragraph 2. *C1*'s life interest under paragraph 2 terminates at his death; it never becomes a present interest.

Stating the bequest in this way, we see that each child's interest in the income consists of two *vested* remainders for life, once each child is born. The "requirement" that each child outlive the other in order to receive another one-half share of the income arises from the fact that there is a cross-remainder *for life* in one-half the income for each child.

The testator, not knowing how many children *A* would have, could not actually have made his bequest in the language of paragraphs 1 and 2. We have simply shown how the language in Example 4-26 is interpreted if two children were born. If *A* had had three (or more) children sharing in the income, we would imply cross-remainders in the same way, although stating them explicitly would be more complex.

The fact that *A* had no children at *T*'s death means that the life estates in the children (including the implied-cross remainders for life) are contingent, but only because they must first be born. *That* contingency is resolved at *A*'s death, so the interest in children is valid.

A different kind of bequest that *T* might make is of the kind we saw in our discussion of gifts to subclasses: the trust principal is divided into shares at *A*'s death, one share for each child, and the principal of a share is distributed at that child's death. (See Example 4-23, § 4.04[A].) That kind of bequest creates no need for implying cross-remainders.

---

[26]*Id.*, § 843, at 335 (2d ed. 1956) states that legal cross-remainders (as opposed to cross-remainders under a trust) will not be implied in a deed.

§ 4.06 Problems for Chapter 4

Are the following interests valid? Answers begin on page   Unless stated otherwise, assume that all persons identified with capital letters are in being (*e.g.*, they survived the testator).

Problem 4-1
T conveys in trust, income to *H* for life, then income to *T*'s children for their lives, and upon the death of the last surviving child, principal to *T*'s grandchildren.

Facts: The trust is irrevocable. At the time of the conveyance, *T* had one child, *C1*, and one grandchild, *G1*. At *T*'s death, *T* had two children, *C1* and *C2*, and two grandchildren, *G1* and *G2*.

Problem 4-2
T makes a bequest in trust, income to *H* for life, then income to *T*'s children for their lives, and upon the death of the last surviving child, principal to *T*'s grandchildren.

Facts: At the time *T*'s will was executed, *T* had one child, *C1*, and one grandchild, *G1*. At *T*'s death, *T* had two children, *C1* and *C2*, and two grandchildren, *G1* and *G2*.

Problem 4-3
T conveys in trust, income to *H* for life, then income to *T*'s children for their lives, and upon the death of the last surviving child, the principal to *T*'s grandchildren.

Facts: The trust is revocable until *T*'s death. At the time of the conveyance, *T* had one child, *C1*, and one grandchild, *G1*. At *T*'s death, *T* had two children, *C1* and *C2*, and two grandchildren, *G1* and *G2*.

Problem 4-4
T makes a bequest to *A* for life, then to *T*'s children for their lives, and upon the death of the last surviving child, to *T*'s grandchildren who reach 21.

Facts: *T* was survived by *A*, children, and one grandchild, *G1*, who was 22 years old.

Problem 4-5
T makes a bequest to *A* for life, then to *A*'s grandchildren.

Facts: *T* was survived by *A* and a child of *A*, *C1*. One of *A*'s grandchildren, *G1*, was alive when *T*'s will was executed but predeceased *T*. *G1* had issue who survived *T*, and they are entitled to take *G1*'s share under the anti-lapse statute.

Problem 4-6
T makes a devise to *A*'s grandchildren who reach 25.

Facts: At *T*'s death, one of *A*'s grandchildren, *G1*, is 25.

Problem 4-7
T makes a devise to *A*'s grandchildren who reach 25.

Facts: By the time of *T*'s death, *A* has had one grandchild, *G1*, age 24.

Problem 4-8
T makes a bequest in trust to pay the income to *H* for life. At the death of *H*, the corpus shall be divided into as many equal shares as there are children of *H* then living. The income from each share shall be paid to the child for whom it is held. At the death of each child, the corpus of his share shall be distributed to his heirs.[27]

Facts: *H* had four children. *C1* and *C2* were born before *T*'s death; *C3* and *C4* were born after *T*'s death.

Problem 4-9
T bequeaths $1,000 to each of *A*'s grandchildren.

Facts: At the time of *T*'s death, *A* had one child, *C1*, and one grandchild, *G1* (*C1*'s child).

Problem 4-10
T bequeaths $1,000 to each of *A*'s grandchildren, whether born before or after *T*'s death.

Facts:
At *T*'s death, the following persons were alive:
 A
 A's child, *C1*
 C1's children, *G1* and *G2*.

After *T*'s death, the following events occurred:
 C1 had another child, *G3*.
 A had another child, *C2*.
 C2 had a child, *G4*.

§ 4.07 Answers to Problems for Chapter 4
Problems begin on page

Answer to Problem 4-1
Since the trust is irrevocable, the perpetuities period starts at the time of the

---

[27]Simplified from *American Security & Trust Co. v. Cramer*, 175 F. Supp. 367 (D.D.C. 1959).

conveyance in trust. The facts at *T*'s death are irrelevant.

Interest in T's children
Step 1. *C1* has a *vested* remainder. However, *T* is alive and can have more children. There is a contingent interest in *T*'s unborn children; the contingency is that they must be born. (There is no condition of survivorship; see the discussion at § 4.05.)

Step 2. *T* is the tentative measuring life. (Since the class closes periodically as the income is paid, there is no person who can serve as another tentative measuring life by closing the class.)

Also, the life estates will fail at the death of the life tenant(s). Therefore, *T*'s children are also tentative measuring lives.

Step 3. *T* was in being. The interest is valid. (*T*'s children were not necessarily all in being, but we already have *T* as the measuring life.)

Interest in T's grandchildren
Step 1. The interest in *G1* is vested. However, more grandchildren of *T* can be born, and there is a contingent interest in them. The contingency is that they must be born. (There is no condition of survivorship.)

Step 2. Grandchildren of *T* can be born as long as there are children of *T* alive. All the children of *T* are the tentative measuring lives.

Step 3. Since *T* is alive, his children are not necessarily all in being. The interests in *T*'s grandchildren, including *G1*'s interest, are invalid.

Step 4. The following could occur:
1. *T* has another child (the "afterborn child").
2. Everyone who was alive when the interest was created dies.
3. Twenty-one years later, the afterborn child is still alive, he could still have a child (who would be a grandchild of *T*), and there is still a contingent interest in the unborn grandchildren of *T*.

Answer to Problem 4-2
The perpetuities period starts when *T*'s will takes effect, at his death.

Interest in T's children
C1 and *C2* have *vested* remainders. (There is no condition of survival; see the discussion at § 4.05.) Their interests are valid. There is no interest in unborn children of *T* because *T* is dead.

Interest in T's grandchildren
Step 1. *G1* and *G2* have vested remainders. However, more grandchildren of *T* can be born, and there is a contingent interest in them. The contingency is that they must be born.

Step 2. Grandchildren of *T* can be born as long as there are children of *T* alive. All the children of *T* are the tentative measuring lives.

Step 3. Since T is dead, all his children are in being. The interest is valid.

Answer to Problem 4-3
The perpetuities period starts when the interests become irrevocable, at T's death. The answer is the same as that for Problem 4-2.

Answer to Problem 4-4
Interest in T's *children*
See the answer to Problem 4-2.

Interest in T's *grandchildren*
Step 1. $G1$ has a vested interest. However, more grandchildren can be born and reach 21.
Contingency #1: Grandchildren must be born.
Contingency #2: They must reach 21.

Step 2.
Contingency #1: Grandchildren of T can be born as long as their parents, children of T, are alive. All the children of T are the tentative measuring lives.

Since there is a birth contingency, we should look for someone who will close the class. At the death of all T's children, the class will close, *if* there is someone who can demand distribution at that time. But we have already chosen T's children as tentative measuring lives, so there is no need to investigate further to see if they work as the "class-closing tentative measuring lives."

Contingency #2: Grandchildren must reach 21. The latest time that a grandchild of T can reach 21 is 21 years after the deaths of the parents, *i.e.*, T's children. They are the tentative measuring lives for this contingency also. (The grandchildren must reach 21, if at all, during their own lifetimes, so they are tentative measuring lives as well.)

Step 3. Since T is dead, all his children are in being. The interest is valid.

Answer to Problem 4-5
Step 1. More grandchildren of A can be born, and they have a contingent interest. The contingency is that they must be born.

Step 2. No grandchildren of A can be born after A's children are dead. All of A's children are tentative measuring lives.

Since we have a birth contingency, we should look for a class-closing tentative measuring life. The class will close at A's death *if* there is someone then alive who can demand distribution of his share. The anti-lapse statute awards $G1$'s share to his issue who survived T. There is no condition of survivorship attached to their interest (except to survive T). Either they, or their heirs or will beneficiaries, will be entitled to demand distribution of their share in the class gift at A's death. The class will surely close at A's death, and A is a "class-closing tentative measuring life."

Step 3. Since *A* is still alive, his children are not necessarily all in being.

The other tentative measuring life is *A*, and he was in being. The interest is valid.

Answer to Problem 4-6
Step 1.
Contingency #1. *A*'s grandchildren must be born.
Contingency #2. *A*'s grandchildren must reach 25.

Step 2.
Contingency #1. *A*'s children are the tentative measuring lives.

Since this is a birth contingency, we see if there is anyone who will close the class. *G1* can demand distribution *now*; the class is closed at *T*'s death. No unborn grandchildren can share in the class gift. Contingency #1 is not, in fact, present.

Contingency #2. *A*'s grandchildren must reach 25. The grandchildren can do so only during their own lives, and they are the tentative measuring lives.

Step 3. More grandchildren of *A* can be born. However, they will not share in the class gift because it has already closed. Those grandchildren of *A* who *can* share in the class gift *are* all in being; *A*'s grandchildren alive at *T*'s death are the measuring lives. The interest is valid.

Answer to Problem 4-7
Step 1.
Contingency #1. *A*'s grandchildren must be born.
Contingency #2. *A*'s grandchildren must reach 25.

Step 2.
Contingency #1. *A*'s children are the tentative measuring lives.

Since this is a birth contingency, we see if there is anyone who will close the class. The class will close as soon as one grandchild reaches 25 and can demand distribution of his share. *G1* may die before reaching 24; there is no one whose death will certainly close the class. We have only *A*'s children as the tentative measuring lives for contingency #1.

Contingency #2: *A*'s grandchildren can reach 25 only during their own lives, and they are the tentative measuring lives.

Step 3. Since *A* is alive, his children are not necessarily all in being. Likewise, *A*'s grandchildren are not necessarily all in being. The interest is invalid.

Step 4. The following could occur:
1. *G1* dies.
2. *A* has another child, *C1*.
3. Everyone who was alive when the interest was created dies.

4. Twenty-one years later, *C1* is still alive, and he could still have a child (*A*'s grandchild) who could reach 25. That grandchild would be entitled to take because the class has not closed. There is still a contingent interest in *A*'s unborn grandchildren.

Answer to Problem 4-8

Interest in H's *children*

Step 1. They must be living at *H*'s death. (They must also be born, but that is implicit in the requirement that they be living at *H*'s death.)

Step 2. *H* is a tentative measuring life. All of *H*'s children are also tentative measuring lives: their life interests will fail at their deaths, and they can satisfy a condition of survivorship only during their lifetimes.

Step 3. *H* was in being. The interest is valid. (*H*'s children are not all in being, but we already have *H* as the measuring life.)

Interest in the heirs of H's *children*

T has not given the entire principal to all the heirs of all the children as one group. Rather, he has given a separate share to the heirs of each child. Therefore, there are *subclasses*, each subclass consisting of the heirs of one child. (It is not entirely clear, however, that the heirs of a person constitute a true class in the first place.) We evaluate each subclass separately.

--Interest in the heirs of C1 *and heirs of* C2

Step 1. The heirs must be ascertained.

Step 2. The heirs of a person are unascertained until that person's death. The contingency will be resolved by the deaths of *C1* and *C2*; they are the tentative measuring lives.

In addition, the size of the share for the subclass of *C1*'s heirs and the size of the share for the subclass of *C2*'s heirs must be fixed within the perpetuities period. That will occur when no more children of *H* can be born, at *H*'s death. *H* is another tentative measuring life.

Step 3. *C1*, *C2*, and *H* were in being. The interests in *C1*'s and *C2*'s heirs are valid.

--Interest in the heirs of each child who was not in being

At the time the interest was created, *C3* and *C4* were not in being, and indeed we could not know whether *H* would have any more children. Therefore, we ought to describe these other subclasses as "the heirs of each child who was not in being at *T*'s death," rather than "the heirs of *C3* and *C4*."

Step 1. The heirs must be ascertained.

Step 2. The heirs of a person are unascertained until that person's death. The contingency will be resolved by the deaths of *H*'s children who were not in being; they are the tentative measuring lives.

Step 3. Obviously, they were not in being. The interest in the heirs of *H*'s children born after *T*'s death is invalid.

Step 4. The following events could occur:
1. *H* has another child (which, in fact happened--he is *C3*).
2. Everyone in the world who was alive when the interest was created dies.
3. Twenty-one years later, *C3* is still alive, and there is still a contingent interest in that child's heirs.

Answer to Problem 4-9

This is a per capita class gift; it closes at *T*'s death (§ 4.01[D][4]). No unborn grandchildren of *A* can share in the gift. The grandchild alive at *T*'s death is entitled to immediate distribution of his share, and his gift is valid.

Answer to Problem 4-10

This is a per capita class gift, but it does not close at *T*'s death, as it normally would, because the testator has expressed a contrary intent. The class will stay open until is biologically closed. The all-or-nothing rule does not apply to a per capita class gift; each grandchild's interest is evaluated separately (§ 4.04[B]). Of course, grandchildren who are in identical circumstances can be treated together.

Interests of G1 *and* G2
Their interests are vested and valid.

Interests of A's *unborn grandchildren whose parent is* C1
C1 had a child, *G3*, who was born after *T*'s death. His circumstances are different from those of *G1* and *G2*, who were in existence at *T*'s death, and therefore we analyze *G3*'s interest separately. The birth of *G3*, occurring as it did after the interests were created, is a fact we cannot take into account. Moreover, the analysis we give here is applicable to anyone in the same circumstances. For these reasons, our heading for this portion of the answer indicates that we are evaluating the interests of *all* of *C1*'s children who could be born after *T*'s death.

Step 1. They must be born.

Step 2. *C1* is the tentative measuring life. (Remember, we are evaluating the interests of only those unborn grandchildren whose parent is *C1*.) Because the class stays open until it is biologically closed, we do not search for a "class-closing tentative measuring life."

Step 3. *C1* was in being. The interest in *A*'s unborn grandchildren whose parent is *C1* is valid. *G3* is one of those grandchildren, and he is entitled to take.

Interests of A's *unborn grandchildren whose parents are unborn children of* A
Both *G3* and *G4* were born after *T*'s death. However, their circumstances differ in that *G3*'s parent was in being at *T*'s death while *G4*'s parent was not. Therefore we must give a different analysis to *G4*'s interest. Both *C2*'s birth and *G4*'s birth are facts that occurred after *T*'s death, so we omit any mention of them in the rest of the analysis. Instead, we say that we are evaluating the interests of all of *A*'s unborn grandchildren (not just *G4*) whose parents are any one of *A*'s unborn children (not just *C2*).

Step 1. They must be born.

Step 2. Their parents, the children of A born after T's death, are the tentative measuring lives.

Step 3. Obviously, those children were not in being. The interest is invalid. $G4$ cannot take.[28]

Step 4. The following events could occur after T's death (in fact, they *did* occur):

1. A has another child.
2. Everyone who was alive when the interest was created dies.
3. Twenty-one years later, that child could still have a child (a grandchild of A). There is still a contingent interest in the grandchildren of A.

---

[28]J. Dukeminier and S. Johanson, Wills, Trusts, and Estates 817 (3d ed. 1984).

Chapter 5
Applying the Rule to powers of appointment

§ 5.01 Review of powers of appointment

A transferor can dispose of his property in an indirect manner by giving *another* person the power to specify the transferees. That power is called a power of appointment.

> **Example 5-1**
> *T* devises Blackacre to *L* for life, then to such persons as *L* shall appoint by will, and in default of appointment, to *L*'s issue then living, per stirpes.

L has the power to determine who shall be the transferee of the remainder in Blackacre; he has a power of appointment. *T* is the *donor*, *L* is the *donee*. "*L*'s issue then living" will take Blackacre if *L* does not exercise the power; they are the *takers in default of appointment*, and their interest is the *gift in default of appointment*. The persons to whom the donee can appoint the property are the *objects* of the power. In the example, *L* can appoint to anyone, but the donor may specify the objects of the power. The person or persons to whom the property is appointed are the *appointees*.

Powers are classified in two ways. A power is *general* or *special* depending on the objects. If the objects include the donee himself, his estate, his creditors, or the creditors of his estate, the power is *general*.[1] Otherwise the power is *special*.

Also, powers are classified by their manner of exercise.

(1) If the donor has specified that the power is to be exercised only by the donee's will, it is a *testamentary power*. (Or we could simply call it a "power to appoint by will.") A donee's exercise of a power by his will is not effective until the will itself becomes effective, at the donee's death.

(2) If the donor has directed that the power is to be exercised during the donee's lifetime or by the donee's will, it is a *power exercisable by deed or will* (also called a *presently exercisable power*).

The donor could direct also that the power can be exercised during the donee's lifetime but not by the donee's will. Such powers are rare; a power exercisable during

---

[1]Our definitions of general and special powers are those used for tax purposes, but they have been widely adopted for general purposes as well. The common-law definitions are slightly different.

the donee's lifetime will be construed to be exercisable by will also unless the donor explicitly says that it is not.[2]

Point of potential confusion
Remember that the labels just discussed refer to the donee, not the donor. A "testamentary" power is a power exercisable by the donee's will, *not* a power created by the donor's will.

---

§ 5.02 In general

When a power of appointment is involved, there are three things to evaluate under the Rule: (1) the power itself, (2) the interests created by exercise of the power, and (3) the gift in default of appointment.

It might be, for example, that a particular power is valid under the Rule, but an interest created by the donee when he exercised the power is not. Of course, if the power itself is invalid under the Rule, then there can be no valid interest created by an attempted exercise of that power.

The way the Rule applies to a power depends on what kind of power it is. General powers exercisable by deed or will are treated in one way; all other powers (*i.e.*, general testamentary powers and all special powers) are treated in a different way.

Note that a power may not be exercisable right away; it can be contingent in the same way that a future interest can be. A power might be contingent because it cannot be exercised until a condition precedent has first been satisfied (for example, "principal to such persons as B shall appoint after B reaches the age of 50"). Or, a power might be contingent because it is given to an unborn or unascertained person; then the power is not exercisable until the person is born or ascertained.[3]

Note also that once a power becomes exercisable, it will remain exercisable for some period of time (except for a testamentary power). It would be possible for the donor to say, for example, that the power expires (is no longer exercisable) when the donee reaches a certain age, or marries, or upon some other event. Almost always, however, a power will remain exercisable until the donee dies, unless he releases it ear-

---

[2]J. Dukeminier and S. Johanson, Wills, Trusts, and Estates 616, n. 3 (3d ed. 1984).

[3]It might not be exercisable until the donee reaches his majority, but that should not make things any more difficult for us. If the Rule is satisfied by the vesting of a future interest in a minor who lacks the capacity to convey the interest, then the Rule ought also to be satisfied by a power becoming "exercisable" in a minor who lacks the capacity to exercise the power. Besides, a child will reach majority--and acquire the capacity to exercise the power--at the end of the 21-year period in gross.

lier. (Of course, once the donee has exercised the power completely--appointed the property--it is no longer exercisable.)

It is this span of time, during which a power will remain in existence and un-exercised, that partly explains why applying the Rule to a power is more complicated than applying the Rule to a future interest. In evaluating a *future interest* under the Rule, there is only one conceptual point in time which is important: when the interest ceases being contingent. In evaluating a *power* under the Rule, there are two points in time which can have importance:

(1) The moment when the power *first becomes* exercisable
(2) The moment when the power *ceases* being exercisable (when it "expires"), usually at the donee's death.

We will have occasion to refer to these two points in time, and the span of time during which a power is exercisable, as we discuss the application of the Rule to powers.

§ 5.03 General powers exercisable by deed or will

[A] Validity of a general power exercisable by deed or will

A donee who has a general power exercisable by deed or will is very close to being the owner of the appointive property. All the donee has to do to own the property is to appoint to himself. For purposes of the Rule, then, we pretend that being able to exercise a general power exercisable by deed or will is equivalent to owning the appointive property. That means that the crucial point in time for evaluating a general power exercisable by deed or will is when it *first* becomes exercisable, *i.e.*, the *beginning* of the span of time to which we referred in § 5.02. The rule is:

> *A general power exercisable by deed or will is valid if it is certain to become exercisable, or fail, within the perpetuities period.* It will be void if there is any possibility that it will first become exercisable beyond the perpetuities period.

The perpetuities period is measured from the time of the creation of the power, just as if the power were a future interest in the donee.

Note carefully that the point in time we are speaking of is when the donee *can* exercise the power, because it is at that time that the donee first becomes, in substance, the owner of the appointive property. It is irrelevant that the donee's *actual* exercise of the power might occur (and does occur) after the end of the perpetuities period.

We have already noted the reasons that a power might not be presently exercisable: there may be a condition precedent or the donee may be unborn or unascertained. Powers which are not yet exercisable for one or more of these reasons should be analyzed under the Rule in the same way that contingent future interests are analyzed.

Example 5-2
Income to *L* for life, then principal to such persons as *L* shall appoint by deed or will, and in default of appointment to *L*'s is-sue then living, per stirpes.

The power is exercisable now, at the time the instrument takes effect. There are no "contingencies" for its exercise, and it is valid.

Example 5-3
Income to L for life, then income to L's first child for life, then principal to such persons as L's first child shall appoint by deed or will, and in default of appointment to L's issue then living, per stirpes.

Facts: L has never had any children.

Step 1 (state the contingencies): Since the power is exercisable by deed or will, it is exercisable as soon as L's first child is born. We state the contingency as "a child of L must be born."

Step 2 (find the tentative measuring lives): L's death resolves the contingency that L's first child must be born.

Step 3 (in being?): L was in being.

The power is valid.

Example 5-4
O conveys in trust, income to his sister Mary for life, then income to Mary's children for their lives, and upon the death of the last surviving child, the principal to such persons as the last surviving child shall appoint by deed or will.[4]

Step 1 (state the contingencies): The donee is the child of Mary who lives the longest. The power will not become exercisable until the donee is ascertained. The contingency is that all but one of Mary's children must die.

Step 2 (find the tentative measuring lives): The deaths of Mary's children (all but the longest-lived one) will resolve the contingency. Mary's children are the tentative measuring lives.

Step 3 (in being?): Since Mary is alive, her children are not necessarily in being. The power is invalid.

Step 4 (construct a counterexample):

1. Mary has two children, $C1$ and $C2$. (These need not be her first two children.)

2. Everyone in the world who was alive when the power was created dies.

---

[4]The conveyance is a simplified version of that in *In re Hargreaves*, 43 Ch.Div. 401 (Court of Appeal 1890).

3. Twenty-one years later, *C1* and *C2* are still alive. We do not know who will live longer. Neither of them qualifies as the donee yet, and neither of them can exercise the power. The power is still not exercisable, and it is invalid.

[B] Validity of interests created by exercise of a general power exercisable by deed or will

We have said that the donee of a general power exercisable by deed or will is treated, for purposes of evaluating the power itself under the Rule, as if he actually owned the appointive property. This treatment applies as well to the validity of the interests created by the exercise of the power.

> *In evaluating interests created by the exercise of a general power exercisable by deed or will, we pretend the donee owned the appointive property and conveyed it to the appointees at the time the power was exercised.*

This means that the perpetuities period starts at the time when the power was *exercised*, not from the time when it was created. To say that the perpetuities period starts when the power was exercised is to say that (1) the persons who serve as measuring lives must be in existence when the power was exercised and (2) the facts that we can take into account in determining what might happen are the facts that were in existence when the power was exercised. But you need not remember all this. Just pretend that the donee owned the property and conveyed it, instead of exercising a power of appointment over the donor's property, and then follow the rules we have been using all along.

Example 5-5
Income to *L* for life, then principal to such persons as *L* shall appoint by deed or will, and in default of appointment to *L*'s issue then living, per stirpes.

Facts: *L* appoints by will to his children for their lives, then upon the death of the last surviving child to his grandchildren.

Since the power is a general power exercisable by deed or will, we pretend that *L*'s exercise of the power was actually a conveyance by him of his property to the appointees.

The interest in *L*'s children consists of present interests and *vested* future interests (see § 4.05); they are valid. We evaluate the contingent interest in *L*'s grandchildren.

Step 1 (state the contingencies): *L*'s grandchildren must be born.

Step 2 (find the tentative measuring lives): The grandchildren's parents, *L*'s children, are the tentative measuring lives.

Step 3 (in being?): Since *L* was dead when he exercised the power, all of *L*'s children were in being. They can serve as measuring lives. The interest in *L*'s grandchildren is valid.

Note that, in Step 3, *L*'s children can serve as measuring lives even though they were not necessarily in being when the power was created. Because we pretend that *L*'s exercise of the power was actually a conveyance by him of the appointive property, the perpetuities period starts when the power was exercised, and it is then that the persons who serve as measuring lives must be in being.

[C] Validity of a gift in default of appointment under a general power exercisable by deed or will

A gift in default of appointment receives treatment consistent with that given the power itself. The takers in default are entitled to possession or enjoyment only by virtue of the donee's failure to exercise the power. If we treat the donee as if he were the owner of the appointive property, then we must treat the takers in default as if they were transferees from the donee, not from the donor. The principle is this:

> *In evaluating an interest which is a gift in default of appointment under a general power exercisable by deed or will, we pretend that the donee transferred the appointive property to the takers in default at the time the power expired unexercised.*[5]

Therefore, the facts that we can take into account are the facts that were in existence when the power expired unexercised, and it is at that time that the measuring lives must be "in being." A power will expire usually at the donee's death or at his release of the power.

Note that this principle is a variation of a doctrine we discussed earlier: an interest that is subject to a power in one person to make himself the absolute owner of the underlying property is not subject to the Rule (§ 3.01[D][2]). The gift in default is subject to the donee's power to make himself the absolute owner of the appointive property by appointing to himself (if it is a general power exercisable by deed or will). Therefore, the gift in default is not subject to the Rule until the power expires. This is what we mean when we say that the perpetuities period does not start until that time.

---

[5]Dukeminier, *Perpetuities: the Measuring Lives*, 85 Columbia L. Rev. 1648, 1670 (1985); Simes & Smith, The Law of Future Interests § 1252 (2d ed. 1956).

Example 5-6
To *A* for life, then to such persons as *A* shall appoint by deed or will; in default of appointment, to *B* for life, then to the first child of *A* to reach 30.[6]

Facts: *A* dies without having exercised the power. No child of *A* has reached the age of 30.

We pretend that *A* has made a devise "to *B* for life, then to the first child of *A* to reach 30" at the time the power expired, at *A*'s death.[7]

Step 1 (state the contingencies): A child of *A* must reach 30.

Step 2 (find the tentative measuring lives): The children of *A* are the tentative measuring lives.

Step 3 (in being?): At the time of *A*'s "devise," *A* was dead, and all his children were in being. The fact that all of *A*'s children were not necessarily in being when the power was created is irrelevant. All of *A*'s children are the measuring lives, and the interest is valid.

§ 5.04 General testamentary powers and special powers

Here we discuss the application of the Rule to general testamentary powers and all special powers (both special testamentary powers and special powers exercisable by deed or will).

[A] Validity of a general testamentary or special power

Unlike the donee of a general power exercisable by deed or will, the donee of a general testamentary or special power is not essentially the owner of the appointive property; he cannot appoint to himself.[8] The important point in time for purposes of the Rule is not when the donee could first exercise the power, but when he could *last* exercise the power. This is the *end* of the span of time described in § 5.02. Therefore:

---

[6]From L. Simes and A. Smith, *The Law of Future Interests* § 1252 at 173-174 (2d ed. 1956).

[7]Of course, if *A* were actually making the conveyance he would say "to *my* first child to reach 30," but this difference in language is without significance.

[8]Actually, one might reasonably think that the donee of a general testamentary power bears a greater resemblance to the donee of a general power exercisable by deed or will (and should be treated in the same way) than to the donee of a special power. But that is not how the law has developed. *See* L. Simes and A. Smith, *The Law of Future Interests* § 1275 (2d ed. 1956).

A general testamentary or special power of appointment is valid if the latest time it could possibly be exercised is within the perpetuities period. It is void if there is any possibility that it will be exercised beyond the perpetuities period.

The perpetuities period is measured from *the time of the creation of the power*, just as if the power were a future interest in the donee.

A power is personal to the donee; if the donee does not exercise the power, it does *not* pass to the donee's heirs or will beneficiaries. Therefore, the donee's lifetime places a limit on the latest time that a power can be exercised. If a power is given to a person who was in being, the power must be good, because the donee can always serve as the measuring life.

Example 5-7
To *L* for life, then to such of *L*'s issue as *L* shall appoint by deed or will, and in default of appointment, to *L*'s issue then living per stirpes.

The donee was in being; therefore the power must be valid. Another, longer, way to reach this result would proceed as follows.

Step 1 (state the contingencies): The latest time the power will be exercisable must fall within the perpetuities period. The latest time the power will be exercisable is at *L*'s death. Therefore, we can state the contingency as "*L* must die."

Step 2 (find the tentative measuring lives): *L* is the tentative measuring life.

Step 3 (in being?): *L* was in being. The power is good.

It is easy to be misled about the validity of a power if it is subject to a condition precedent.

Example 5-8
To *A*, but if a child of *A* is convicted of a crime, then *B* may appoint the property among his issue.

The donee was in being; therefore the power must be valid. It is true that the power is subject to a condition precedent that is too remote: the only persons whose deaths resolve the contingency of a child of *A* being convicted of a crime are *A*'s children, and they are not necessarily all in being. But that is irrelevant, because the latest time the power can be exercised is at *B*'s death (the power is personal to *B*), and *B* can serve as the measuring life.[9]

If, instead, *B*'s power was a general power exercisable by deed or will, it would be valid as well. Even though we cannot be certain that the power would first become exercisable within the perpetuities period, it would fail (expire) at the death of *B* (a

---

[9]L. Simes and A. Smith, The Law of Future Interests § 1272, at 208 (2d ed. 1956).

person in being) if had not been exercised by that time. That is enough to satisfy the Rule.

But any general testamentary or special power is void if it is given to an unborn person, unless its exercise is specially restricted. The exercise would be specially restricted if, for example, the donee could exercise the power no later than 21 years after *A*'s death; if *A* were in being, the power would be good. But that kind of power is very unusual. The latest time that an *un*restricted power can be exercised is at the donee's death (or just before the donee's death, if the donor has explicitly stated that a special power exercisable by deed is not exercisable by will). The donee's death will fall beyond the perpetuities period if the donee is unborn. The following example illustrates the point.

> **Example 5-9**
> Income to *L* for life, then income to *L*'s first child for his life, then principal to such persons as *L*'s first child shall appoint by will, and in default of appointment, to *L*'s issue then living, per stirpes.
>
> Facts: *L* has had no children.

The latest time that the power can be exercised (and, in fact, the only time) is at the death of *L*'s first child, when his will becomes effective. *L*'s first child is the tentative measuring life, but he was not in being. There is no one in being whose death has any effect on the death of *L*'s first child, so no one else resolves the "contingency." The power is invalid.

Discretionary trusts

If a trustee has the discretion to distribute trust income or principal to trust beneficiaries, then the trustee is considered to have a special power of appointment for purposes of the Rule against Perpetuities. A corporate trustee, of course, has an indefinite lifespan; and an individual trustee will be replaced, at his death, by a successor trustee (appointed by a court, if necessary).[10] A trustee, then, has no "lifetime" which would limit the exercise of a power of appointment. The only limitations on the exercise of a power held by a trustee, then, are the lifetimes of the persons to whom the property can be appointed. Once they have died, the power is no longer exercisable. If the persons to whom the trustee can distribute trust income or principal (*i.e.*, the objects of the power) were in being, the power is valid. If they were not in being, the power is invalid, in whole or in part,[11] unless the power is specially restricted. The power would be restricted if, for example, the trustee was directed to make distributions only until the unborn beneficiary reached 21, and the beneficiary's parent was in being. In that case the power would be valid.

---

[10]The result would be otherwise if the settlor intended the discretion to distribute trust income or principal to be personal to the original individual trustee.

[11]The law is not clear on this point. *See* 6 American Law of Property § 24.32, at 96 (A. Casner ed. 1952); L. Simes and A. Smith, The Law of Future Interests § 1277, at 217 (2d ed. 1956).

Example 5-10

T makes a bequest in trust, the trustee to distribute so much of the income to *T*'s children as the trustee in its discretion determines, and to add to principal the income not so distributed (with additional provisions for distribution of the principal).

The power cannot be exercised beyond the lifetimes of the objects, *T*'s children. They are the tentative measuring lives. Since *T* is dead, all of *T*'s children are in being. The power is good.

Example 5-11

T makes a bequest in trust, to pay so much of the income and principal as the trustee deems necessary to the issue of *T*'s son who were born within 20 years of *T*'s death. The trust shall continue for as long as there are such issue alive; when all of such issue have died, the trustee shall distribute the principal to *T*'s issue then living.

The power is exercisable for as long as the specified issue are alive. They are not necessarily in being, and they cannot serve as measuring lives. The power is invalid.[12]

[B] Validity of interests created by exercise of a general testamentary or special power[13]

Here the donee is treated, not as if he were the owner of the appointive property, as in the case of a general power exercisable by deed or will, but as the donor's "agent" in filling in blanks in the donor's instrument.[14] We refer back to the instrument which created the power and mentally insert the interests which the donee created when he exercised the power. Then we evaluate those interests as if the donor had made them in the first place. In short:

> *In evaluating an interest which was created by the exercise of a general testamentary or special power of appointment, we pretend that the donor created the interests at the time he created the power (subject, however, to the "second look" doctrine, below).*

---

[12]*Thomas v. Harrison*, 191 N.E.2d 862 (Probate Court of Ohio, Cuyahoga County 1962).

[13]We assume here and in the problems that the donee of a special power may appoint in further trust.

[14]Dukeminier, *Perpetuities: the Measuring Lives*, 85 Columbia L. Rev. 1648, 1670 (1985).

The second look doctrine

There is a twist to this, however. Since we pretend that the donor created the interests, normally we would say that the perpetuities period "starts" at the time the instrument executed by the donor took effect. And, to say that the perpetuities period "starts" at that time normally means two things:

(1) The persons who serve as measuring lives must be in being at that time.

(2) The facts we are entitled to take into account in determining what might happen concerning vesting and failing are those facts that were in existence at that time.

When we evaluate interests created by exercise of a general testamentary or special power, however, *only (1) holds true; (2) does not. The measuring lives must be in being when the donor created the power*, as usual. But we do not know what the appointed interests are until the donee exercises the power. Therefore, in determining "what might happen," *we are entitled to take into account facts that existed at the time the donee exercised the power.* This is known as the "second look" doctrine--it allows us to take another look at the facts partway into the perpetuities period.

> **Example 5-12**
> *T* makes a devise to *A* for life, then to such of *A*'s issue as he shall appoint by deed or will, and in default of appointment, to *A*'s issue then living, per stirpes.
>
> Facts: In his will, *A* appoints to his children for their lives, then upon the death of the last surviving child to his grandchildren. *A* had two children, *C1* and *C2*, who were alive at *T*'s death and were still alive at the time *A* exercised the power.[15]

We rewrite *T*'s devise so that it reflects the appointment which *A* has made: "to *A* for life, then to *A*'s children for their lives, then upon the death of the last surviving child to *A*'s grandchildren."

Let us evaluate the interest in *A*'s grandchildren.

Step 1 (state the contingencies): *A*'s grandchildren must be born.

Step 2 (find the tentative measuring lives): *C1* and *C2* are the tentative measuring lives. Normally we would say that *all* of *A*'s children are the tentative measuring lives. But the second look doctrine allows us to take into account all facts existing at the time of the appointment. At that time, A was dead, and *C1* and *C2* were the only children that *A* would ever have. We can identify them as the measuring lives.

Step 3 (in being?): *C1* and *C2* were alive at *T*'s death. They work as measuring lives, and the interest in *A*'s grandchildren is valid.

---

[15]Adapted from J. Dukeminier and S. Johanson, Wills, Trusts, and Estates 824 (3d ed. 1984).

The interest in *A*'s children is valid even without the aid of the second look doctrine; *A* is the measuring life (see also § 4.05).

[C] Validity of a gift in default of appointment under a general testamentary or special power

The gift in default of appointment is an interest created by the donor, and therefore it should be treated in the same way as any other interest created in the donor's instrument. That means that the perpetuities period runs from the time the donor's instrument took effect.

A gift in default of appointment does not take effect unless the power is not exercised. However, the non-exercise of the power is *not* thought of as a condition precedent to the gift in default of appointment. Rather, the *exercise* of the power is considered to be a divesting condition (condition subsequent) to which the gift in default of appointment is subject. Therefore, the gift in default of appointment will be vested (subject to divestment) unless it is given to an unborn/unascertained person or is subject to a condition precedent.

<u>Does the second-look doctrine apply?</u>
There is one thing that is not clear regarding application of the Rule to a gift in default of appointment under a general testamentary or special power: whether the second-look doctrine applies. On the one hand, it seems that the gift in default of appointment is not "really" made until the power expires without the donee having exercised it. Therefore, the reasoning goes, the second-look doctrine ought to apply to the gift in default of appointment in approximately the same way that it applies to interests created by exercise of the power. That would mean that, although the perpetuities period runs from the creation of the power, we are entitled to look at facts in existence at the time the power expires. There is a Massachusetts case which has endorsed this reasoning,[16] and Professor Leach approves of it,[17] as apparently does Professor Dukeminier.[18]

On the other hand, Professors Simes and Smith maintain that the Massachusetts case is wrongly decided and that most courts would hold the second-look doctrine *not* to apply to the gift in default of appointment, although their treatise cites no cases clearly so holding.[19] Under this view, we treat the gift in default of appointment exactly as we treat any other interest created in the donor's instrument. The period runs

---

[16]*Sears v. Coolidge*, 329 Mass. 340, 108 N.E.2d 563 (1952).

[17]6 American Law of Property § 24.24, at 78 (1952).

[18]Dukeminier, *Perpetuities: the Measuring Lives*, 85 Columbia L. Rev. 1648, 1671 (1985).

[19]L. Simes and A. Smith, The Law of Future Interests § 1276, at 215 (2d ed. 1956).

from the date when the instrument took effect, and we can take into account only the facts existing at that time.

§ 5.05 Problems for Chapter 5

Are the following powers and interests valid? Unless stated otherwise, assume that all persons identified with capital letters are in being (*e.g.*, they survived the testator). Answers begin on page

Problem 5-1

T makes a bequest in trust, income to *A* for life, then income to *B*'s first child for life, then principal to such persons as *B*'s first child shall appoint by deed or will.

Facts: By the time of *T*'s death, *B* had not had any children. Later, *B*'s first child appoints by will to *C* for life, then to *C*'s children. *C* was born after *T*'s death but before the death of *B*'s first child.

Problem 5-2

T makes a devise to *A*, but when one of *B*'s children marries, then *B* may appoint to any person by deed or will.

Problem 5-3

Income to *L* for life, then income to *L*'s children for their lives, then upon the death of the last surviving child the principal to such of *L*'s issue as the last surviving child shall appoint by deed or will.

Facts: *L*'s last surviving child, *C1*, appoints to his daughter.

Problem 5-4

T makes a devise to *A* for life, then to such of *A*'s issue as he shall appoint by will.

Facts: *A* appoints to his children for their lives, then upon the death of the last surviving child to *A*'s grandchildren. *A* had two children, *C1* and *C2*, both of whom survived him. *C1* was born before *T*'s death; *C2* was born after *T*'s death.

Problem 5-5

T makes a devise to *A* for life, then to such of *A*'s issue as he shall appoint by will.

Facts: *A* appoints to his children for their lives, then upon the death of the last surviving child to *A*'s grandchildren. *A* had two children, *C1* and *C2*. *C1* was born before *T*'s death and survived *A*. *C2* was born after *T*'s death and predeceased *A*.

Problem 5-6
T makes a devise to *A* for life, then to such of *A*'s issue as he shall appoint by will.

Facts: *A* appoints to his child *C1* for life, then to *C1*'s children. *C1* was born after *T*'s death and survived *A*.

§ 5.06 Answers to Problems for Chapter 5

Problems begin on page

Answer to Problem 5-1
Validity of the power
Step 1. The power is a general power exercisable by deed or will. It must become exercisable within the period. That will occur when *B*'s first child is born. The contingency is that *B*'s first child must be born.

Step 2. *B* is the tentative measuring life.

Step 3. *B* was in being at *T*'s death. The power is valid.

Validity of the interests created by exercise of the power
We pretend that *B*'s first child made a devise to *C* for life, then to *C*'s children.

--Interest in C
C's interest vested immediately; it is valid.

--Interest in C's children
Step 1. They must be born.
Step 2. *C* is the tentative measuring life.
Step 3. *C* was in being at the time of the appointment (*B*'s first child's death). The interest is valid.

Answer to Problem 5-2
Validity of the power
The power is in a living person and is valid. Or, we can do the full analysis:
Step 1. The power is a general power exercisable by deed or will and must become exercisable, or fail, within the period. The contingency for its exercise is that one of *B*'s children must marry.

Step 2. *B*'s children are the tentative measuring lives.
However, the power will *fail* when the donee dies. Therefore, *B* is another tentative measuring life.

Step 3. Since *B* is alive, his children are not necessarily all in being. However, *B* is in being, and the power is valid.

Answer to Problem 5-3
Validity of the power
The power is a special power of appointment given to a potentially unborn person; it is invalid. More completely:

Step 1. The last time the power is exercisable must not be beyond the perpetuities period. It will be exercisable until the death of the last surviving child of *L*. The contingency is that he must die.

Step 2. The tentative measuring life is the last surviving child of *L*.

Step 3. Since *L* is alive, his last surviving child was not necessarily in being. The power is invalid.

Validity of the interests created by exercise of the power
Since the power is invalid, any attempted exercise of the power is of no effect.

Answer to Problem 5-4
Validity of the power
The donee is in being, so the power must be good. The full analysis is as follows:

Step 1. The power is a special power. The last time it is exercisable must not be beyond the perpetuities period. The last (and only) time it is exercisable is at *A*'s death. The contingency is that *A* must die.

Step 2. *A* is the tentative measuring life.

Step 3. *A* was in being. The power is valid.

Validity of the interests created by exercise of the power
Since the power is a special power, we pretend that the donor created the interests at the time the power was created. It as if *T* made a devise to *A* for life, then to *A*'s children for their lives, then upon the death of the last surviving child to *A*'s grandchildren.

--Interest in A's children
Step 1. Under the second-look doctrine, we can take into account the fact that the interest vested immediately upon exercise of the power, at *A*'s death. Alternatively, we can say that the contingency is that *A*'s children must be born.

Step 2. Under either analysis, *A* is the tentative measuring life.

Step 3. *A* was in being at *T*'s death. The interest is valid.

--Interest in A's grandchildren
Step 1. The grandchildren must be born.

Step 2. *C1* and *C2* are the tentative measuring lives. Under the second look doctrine, we can take into account that *C1* and *C2* are the only children *A* ever had (*A* was dead at the time of the appointment).

Step 3. The perpetuities period starts at the time of *T*'s death, and *C1* and *C2* must have been in being at that time. *C2* was not then in being, and the interest in grandchildren is invalid.

Step 4. The following events could occur after *A*'s appointment. Remember that we are pretending that the donor, *T*, created the interest in *A*'s grandchildren.

1. Everyone who was alive when the interest was created (at *T*'s death) dies. (Note that this group does not include *C2*.)
2. Twenty-one years later, *C2* (who was not in being) is still alive and can still have a child (a grandchild of *A*). There is still a contingent interest in *A*'s grandchildren. (The interest in the grandchildren whose parent is *C1* is bad because of the all-or-nothing rule; there is not an adequate indication of subclasses here.)

Answer to Problem 5-5
Validity of the power
See answer to Problem 5-4.

Validity of the interests created by exercise of the power
Since the power is a special power, we pretend that the donor created the appointed interests at the time the power was created. It as if *T* made a devise to *A* for life, then to *A*'s children for their lives, then upon the death of the last surviving child to *A*'s grandchildren.

--Interest in A's children
See answer to Problem 5-4.

--Interest in A's grandchildren
Step 1. The grandchildren must be born.

Step 2. Under the second look doctrine, we can take into account that *C1* and *C2* are the only children *A* ever had (*A* was dead at the time of the appointment). Further, we are entitled to take into account the fact that *C2* predeceased *A*. That means that *C1* is the only tentative measuring life we need. *C1* can serve as a tentative measuring life for his own children, of course. But *C1* can also serve as the tentative measuring life for *C2*'s children: at the time of the appointment, *C2* is dead, *C1* is still alive, and we know that none of *C2*'s children will be born after *C1*'s death. Or, *A* could serve as the tentative measuring life for *C2*'s children, since we know by the time of the appointment that none of *C2*'s children can be born after *A*'s death. We do not want to use *C2* himself as a tentative measuring life because he was not in being at *T*'s death.

Step 3. *C1* and *A* were in being at *T*'s death. The interest is valid.

Answer to Problem 5-6
Validity of the power
See answer to Problem 5-4.

Validity of the interests created by exercise of the power

Since the power is a special power, we rewrite T's devise so that it reflects the appointment which A has made: to A for life, then to $C1$ for life, then to $C1$'s children.

--Interest in C1

Step 1. Under the second-look doctrine, we know that $C1$'s interest vested immediately upon exercise of the power, at A's death. Alternatively, we can say that the contingency is that $C1$ must be born.

Step 2. Under either analysis, A is the tentative measuring life.

Step 3. A was in being. $C1$'s interest is valid.

--Interest in C1*'s children*

Step 1. They must be born.

Step 2. $C1$ is the tentative measuring life.

Step 3. $C1$ was not in being at T's death. The interest is invalid.

Step 4. The following sequence of events could (and did) occur:
1. After T's death, A has a child (he was $C1$).
2. Everyone who was alive at T's death dies.
3. Twenty-one years later, $C1$ is still alive, and he can still have a child. There is still a contingent interest in $C1$'s children.

If $C1$ had been in existence at T's death, he could have served as the measuring life, and the interest in $C1$'s children would have been valid. Even if $C1$ had not been in existence at T's death, if he had predeceased A, then the interest would have been valid; A would have been the measuring life.[20] (Compare Problem 5-5.)

---

[20]T. Bergin and P. Haskell, *Preface to Estates in Land and Future Interests* 201-202 (2d ed. 1984); Leach, *Perpetuities in a Nutshell*, 51 Harv. L. Rev. 638, 653 (1938).

Chapter 6
Miscellaneous

§ 6.01 Infectious invalidity

We know that the Rule applies separately to each interest; the invalidity of one interest under the Rule does not affect the validity of another interest in the same instrument. (Recall, however, that the invalidity of one interest may "change" another interest in the same instrument. See Example 3-19, § 3.08[C][1], and Example 3-21, § 3.08[C][2].)

However, the *transferor's presumed intent* might require that another interest be declared invalid. Under the doctrine of infectious invalidity, a court might decide that the transferor's attempted scheme of disposition is so disrupted by the invalidity of one interest that the transferor would not have wanted other interests (or the entire conveyance) to stand.

If the court thinks the doctrine of infectious invalidity should *not* apply, the court will sometimes say that it is applying the opposite doctrine of "separability"; the valid interests are "separable" from the invalid one.

§ 6.02 Options

An option to purchase land may be part of a lease of the land (the lessee being the person holding the option) or not. In the latter case, the option is said to be "in gross."

In the large majority of states,[1] an option in gross is subject to the Rule. Thus, if there is any possibility that the option will be exercised beyond the perpetuities period, it is void. If the option is personal to the person holding the option, it will be valid: it cannot be exercised after his death, and he can serve as the measuring life.

If the grantor of land retains an option to repurchase it, that option is subject to the Rule, just like any other option in gross. That is so even though an option in the grantor looks very much like a right of entry, which is not subject to the Rule.

---

[1]J. Dukeminier and S. Johanson, Wills, Trusts, and Estates 784 (3d ed. 1984).

If an option to purchase land is part of a lease of that land, however, it is not subject to the Rule.[2] Likewise, an option in a lease to renew the lease, even perpetually, is not subject to the Rule.[3]

§ 6.03 Splitting the contingencies (alternative gifts)

An interest which will vest upon *either one* of two events, stated separately, is treated as two separate interests.

Example 6-1
To *A*, but if *A* has no children, or if none of *A*'s children marries, to *B*.

The transferor has said that *B*'s interest will vest, and *B* will be entitled to possession, if *either* one of two contingencies is satisfied. Therefore, *B* is considered to have *two* interests, or "alternative gifts." The gift that is subject to the condition that none of *A*'s children marries is void under the Rule, because the contingency will not be resolved until the deaths of all of *A*'s children, who were not necessarily in being. The gift that is subject to the condition that *A* have no children is valid, however, because that contingency will be resolved at *A*'s death, and *A* was in being. Therefore, *B* will take if *A* dies without having had any children.

Example 6-2
To *A*, but if *A* has no children who marry, to *B*.

The contingency "if *A* has no children who marry" will be satisfied if either of two things happens: (1) *A* has no children at all, or (2) he has children but none of them marries. Therefore, this conveyance seems to give *B* exactly the same interests he had in the preceding example. The crucial difference is that in the preceding example the transferor *expressly* stated two different contingecies, while in this example he has stated only *one*. We cannot "split" this single contingency when the transferor has failed to do so, and *B* has but *one* interest in this example. The contingency might not be resolved until the deaths of all of *A*'s children, who were not in being, and the interest in *B* is invalid. Even if *A* dies without having had any children, *B* takes nothing.

§ 6.04 Avoiding invalidity under the Rule by appropriate construction

Professor Gray states that we must construe the language of an instrument first, without regard to the possible invalidity of an interest under the Rule, and then

---

[2]L. Simes and A. Smith, The Law of Future Interests § 1244, at 162 (2d ed. 1956). However, Leach, *Perpetuities in a Nutshell*, 51 Harv. L. Rev. 638, 661 (1938), maintains that the courts are split on the point.

[3]L. Simes and A. Smith, The Law of Future Interests § 1243 (2d ed. 1956); Leach, *Perpetuities in a Nutshell*, 51 Harv. L. Rev. 638, 662 (1938).

"remorselessly" apply the Rule.[4] Many courts have agreed. On the other hand, there are several ways by which the Rule might be avoided by apt construction, and some courts have done just that, apparently ignoring Professor Gray's advice.

[A] Construction of an interest as vested rather than contingent

> **Example 6-3**
> *T* makes a bequest to the children of *A* if they reach 25, but if no child of *A* reaches 25, then to *B*.[5]
>
> Facts: No child of *A* has yet reached 25.

If the interest in *A*'s children is contingent on their reaching 25, their interest is invalid. Because of the strong preference for vested interests, however, the words "if they reach 25" would probably be ignored as surplusage. The condition subsequent, "but if no child of A reaches 25," will not be resolved within the perpetuities period; the condition and *B*'s interest are void. The interest in *A*'s children is still contingent on their being born, but that will be resolved by the time of *A*'s death, who can serve as the measuring life. (See § 3.08[C][2].)

> **Example 6-4**
> To *A*'s first child, to be paid at the age of 25.
>
> Facts: *A* has had no children.

If the interest in *A*'s first child were subject to a condition precedent that he reach 25, it would be invalid. But the "to be paid" language is construed to postpone the time of payment only, not the vesting of the interest (see § 2.04[C][1]). The interest vests as soon as the child is born, which will occur not later than *A*'s death. *A* is the measuring life, and the interest is valid.

[B] A general description includes only persons in existence when the instrument was executed

> **Example 6-5**
> *T* makes a bequest in trust to pay the income to *A* for his life, then to pay the income to *A*'s children for their lives, then upon the death of the last surviving child to pay the principal to *A*'s grandchildren.
>
> Facts: *A* has two children, *C1* and *C2*.

---

[4] J. Gray, The Rule Against Perpetuities § 629 (4th ed. 1942).

[5] From 6 American Law of Property § 24.19, at 60-61 (A. Casner ed. 1952).

The interest in *A*'s grandchildren is invalid because our tentative measuring lives, all of *A*'s children, were not necessarily in being. However, suppose that *C1* and *C2* were in existence at the time the will was executed and that *A* was then sufficiently old that *T* probably did not expect him to have more children. In that case, a court might say that *T* intended the words "*A*'s children" to refer only to *C1* and *C2* and the words "*A*'s grandchildren" to refer only to children of *C1* and *C2*. Then the interest in the grandchildren would be valid, because *C1* and *C2* could serve as the measuring lives.

Similarly, a reference to a son's widow (Example 3-22, § 3.09[A]) might be construed to mean the son's present wife.

[C] An event that might not happen for an indefinite time must occur within a reasonable time

We saw that an interest which is contingent on distribution of the testator's estate is invalid because we cannot know when that might occur (§ 3.09[B]). But a court might conclude that the testator meant for the interest to remain contingent until distribution only if distribution of the estate takes place within a reasonable time, and a reasonable time is less than the 21-year period in gross under the Rule.[6] Other apparently indefinite contingencies might be given a similar construction.[7]

§ 6.05 Applying the Rule if the doctrine of destructibility of contingent remainders is in force

The doctrine of destructibility of contingent remainders is in force in only a few states.[8] Where it still operates, a legal contingent remainder in land will *fail* if it has not vested by the time the preceding estate has ended. (The doctrine does not apply to executory interests.) The doctrine affords us an alternative way of failing which

---

[6]See *Belfield v. Booth*, 63 Conn. 299, 27 A. 585 (1893).

[7]*E.g., Omath Holding Co. v. City of New York*, 523 N.Y.S.2d 969 (Sup. 1988) (lease to begin 42 months after the property was rezoned contains an implied requirement that the rezoning be accomplished within a reasonable period, which is less than 21 years); *Wong v. DiGrazia*, 60 Cal. 2d 525, 386 P.2d 817 (1963) (contract which provided that a lease of a building was to begin when construction was completed contains an implied condition that construction be completed within a reasonable time, which is less than 21 years).

[8]According to Powell, it is "reasonably certain" that the doctrine is in force in Florida, Oregon, Pennsylvania, and Tennessee, while dicta in Arkansas, North Carolina, and South Carolina cases indicate the doctrine exists in those states. 2A R. Powell, Real Property 314 (P. Rohan rev. ed. 1982). However, Professor Dukeminier concludes that Arkansas and Tennessee have repudiated destructibility, and he points out that among the states on Powell's list only Florida has a case less than 60 years old which recognizes the doctrine. Dukeminier, *Contingent Remainders and Executory Interests: A Requiem for the Distinction*, 43 Minn. L. Rev. 13, 34-36 (1958); J. Dukeminier and S. Johanson, Wills, Trusts, and Estates 702 (3d ed. 1984).

can help us in selecting tentative measuring lives. As a result, some interests which are invalid under the Rule against Perpetuities in states where remainders are no longer destructible are valid in states where the doctrine is still in force.

Example 6-6
To *A* for life, then to *B*'s first child, if he reaches the age of 30.

Facts: *B* has never had any children.

Step 1 (state the contingencies):
Contingency #1. A child of *B* must be born.
Contingency #2. He must reach 30.

Step 2 (find the tentative measuring lives): As for the first contingency, *B* is the tentative measuring life. As for the second contingency, *B*'s first child is the tentative measuring life.

If the doctrine of destructibility of contingent remainders is in force, there is an alternative way of failing. The remainder will *fail* if it has not vested by the time *A*'s life estate ends. Therefore, *A*'s death will resolve both contingencies, and *A* is another tentative measuring life.

Step 3 (in being?): *B* is in being, so the first contingency does not cause us any problems. As for the second contingency: *B*'s first child is not in being. *A*, however, is in being, and he qualifies as a measuring life. The remainder is valid in a state where remainders are destructible but invalid where the doctrine is no longer in force.

We might have said, more briefly, that under the doctrine of destructibility of contingent remainders, a remainder cannot still be contingent when the preceding life estate ends, so obviously *A* serves as a measuring life.

Suppose that *B* has a child, *C1*, who had not yet reached the age of 30 by the time of *A*'s death. Under these facts, it does not matter whether or not we are in a state where the doctrine of destructibility of contingent remainders is in force. In a state which does not recognize the doctrine, *C1*'s interest will be invalid under the Rule against Perpetuities. In a state which recognizes the doctrine, his interest will be valid under the Rule against Perpetuities, but it will fail at *A*'s death because it had not yet vested.

On the other hand, suppose that *B*'s first child, *C1*, is 30 at *A*'s death. In a state which does not recognize destructibility of contingent remainders, his interest is invalid under the Rule against Perpetuities and he takes nothing. In a state which does recognize the doctrine, *C1*'s interest is valid under the doctrine and under the Rule against Perpetuities; he will be entitled to possession at *A*'s death.

Chapter 7
Modifications of the common-law Rule

§ 7.01 "Wait and see"

The essence of the common-law Rule against Perpetuities is its concern with what *might* happen, not what *did* happen. Even if a contingent interest vested very soon after its creation, it is invalid if there was any possibility that it could have remained contingent beyond the perpetuities period.

This fundamental aspect of the common-law Rule is reversed under the wait-and-see doctrine, which by one count has been adopted, in various degrees, in almost half the states by statute or judicial decision.[1] If an interest is *invalid* under the common-law Rule, we apply the wait-and-see rule by waiting until the end of the perpetuities period to see if it actually *did* vest by then. If it did, it is valid. The fact that it might have remained contingent beyond the perpetuities period is irrelevant. Any interest which is *valid* under the common-law Rule is also valid in states that have adopted the wait-and-see rule.[2]

But the "perpetuities period" is different under the wait-and-see rule, because the concept of the measuring lives is different. Under the common-law rule, the measuring lives are persons whose deaths resolve the contingencies immediately or within 21 years. If an interest is *invalid* under the common-law rule, then no such person exists. But it is precisely when an interest is invalid under the common-law Rule that the wait-and-see rule requires us to wait until the end of the "perpetuities period" to see if the interest has vested. Since we cannot select a measuring life in the usual way, the wait-and-see rule must *tell us* who the measuring lives are.[3]

Depending on the particular wait-and-see rule, the measuring lives may be the transferees of preceding life estates, or the transferees of preceding life estates plus additional persons who are selected very much as we have selected tentative measuring lives, or various persons who have some connection with the interest (though the connection in some cases can be rather remote).[4]

---

[1]Dukeminier, *Perpetuities: the Measuring Lives*, 85 Columbia L. Rev. 1648, 1655 (1985).

[2]*Id.* at 1656.

[3]*See* J. Dukeminier and S. Johanson, Wills, Trusts, and Estates 847 (3d ed. 1984).

[4]This last method is in the Restatement (Second) of Property, Donative Transfers § 1.4 (1983), which gives a list of the measuring lives.

§ 7.02   Equitable reformation (cy pres)

In a few cases the courts have been willing to reform an instrument to avoid violation of the Rule.

> **Example 7-1**
> To *A* for life, then to the first child of *A* to reach the age of 30.
>
> Facts: No child of *A* has reached the age of 30.

The remainder is invalid under the Rule (see Example 3-8, § 3.07[C]). The difficulty, of course, is that the age contingency is 9 years too long. However, some courts would reform the instrument to reduce the age contingency to 21, resulting in a valid interest. In addition, some states have statutes authorizing reformation.

§ 7.03   The rule against suspension of the power of alienation

In a few states, a rule "against suspension of the power of alienation" is in force instead of, or in addition to, the Rule against Perpetuities. The rule against suspension of the power of alienation differs from the common-law Rule primarily in *what must happen* within the perpetuities period.[5] What the common-law Rule demands is the vesting or failing of a contingent interest within the perpetuities period. By contrast, the rule against suspension of the power of alienation requires, as its name suggests, that any "suspension of the power of alienation" end within the perpetuities period. The power of alienation is *present* (not suspended) if everyone who owns an interest in the underlying property could convey his interest to one transferee and thereby create in him a present possessory fee simple absolute. The power of alienation is *suspended* when that cannot be done.

Under what circumstances would the power of alienation be suspended? Every kind of interest in property, present or future, can be assigned or released by its owner. (A right of entry, for example, may not be alienable inter-vivos, but it would still be releasable to the owner of the estate on condition subsequent.) Therefore, it would always be possible for all the owners of all future interests to assign or release their interests to one person unless *a future interest is owned by an unborn or unascertained person*, who obviously could not assign or release his interest. The rule against suspension of the power of alienation is violated, therefore, *if there is the possibility that a future interest will remain in an unborn or unascertained person for longer than the perpetuities period*. The rule would be violated also if the alienation of an interest were explicitly prohibited for longer than the period.

> **Example 7-2**
> To *A*, but if the land ceases to be used for church purposes, to *B*.

---

[5]The perpetuities period may be different as well.

The owners of all interests (*A* and *B*) are born and ascertained. *A* and *B* could convey their interests to a transferee, who would then have the present possessory fee simple absolute. *B*'s interest is valid under the rule against suspension of the power of alienation, although it would be void under the Rule against Perpetuities.

Example 7-3
To *A* for life, then to *A*'s first grandchild.

Facts: *A* has had no grandchildren.

The interest in *A*'s first grandchild will be inalienable, and the power of alienation will be suspended, until he is born. That "contingency" will not be resolved until the deaths of *A*'s children, who are not necessarily all in being. The power of alienation will be suspended for longer than the perpetuities period, and the interest in *A*'s first grandchild is invalid.

Under the common-law Rule against Perpetuities, an interest is invalid if it might remain contingent beyond the perpetuities period, and an interest is contingent if it is subject to a condition precedent *or* if it is given to an unborn/unascertained person. Under the rule against suspension of the power of alienation, on the other hand, an interest is invalid if it is given to someone who might remain unborn/unascertained for longer than the period. You can see that every interest that is valid under the common-law Rule will also be valid under the rule against suspension of the power of alienation, unless alienation is specially restricted.

§ 7.04 The Uniform Statutory Rule Against Perpetuities

In 1986 the National Conference of Commissioners on Uniform State Laws approved a Uniform Statutory Rule Against Perpetuities.[6] The chief changes to the common-law Rule made by the USRAP are the creation of a 90-year period in gross for vesting and a wait-and-see component. Under the USRAP, an interest is valid if it is valid under the common-law rule *or* if it *actually* vests within 90 years after its creation.

---

[6]8A U.L.A. 103 (Supp. 1988).

Chapter 8
Related rules

§ 8.01 Duration of trusts

The Rule against Perpetuities does not require that a trust terminate within the perpetuities period; it merely requires that all interests under the trust must necessarily vest (or fail) within that time. However, there is a restriction, very much like the Rule against Perpetuities, which limits the duration of a trust: a trust cannot remain indestructible for longer than the perpetuities period. A trust is indestructible if the beneficiaries cannot require distribution of the trust corpus and termination of the trust, and they cannot do so if that would interfere with the accomplishment of a material purpose of the settlor (for example, the support of a life income beneficiary).

A settlor may direct that property be held in "trust" for the upkeep of his tomb or for the care of an animal. Such an arrangement is called an honorary trust. Obviously there are no beneficiaries who can demand its termination, and it is void if there is a possibility that it might last longer than the perpetuities period.[1]

A charitable trust is not subject to any rule limiting the duration of trusts; it is valid although it can last forever.

§ 8.02 Accumulation of income

A settlor may direct that the trustee accumulate income and continue to hold it in trust for later distribution. A provision that income be accumulated for a period that is longer than the perpetuities period is void, either entirely or for the excess period, unless the accumulation is for charitable purposes.[2] In addition, some states have statutes prohibiting accumulations for longer than the perpetuities period.

---

[1]L. Simes and A. Smith, The Law of Future Interests 248 (2d ed. 1956).

[2]T. Bergin and P. Haskell, Preface to Estates in Land and Future Interests 222, 224 (2d ed. 1984).